# Nahanni Trailhead

# NAHANNI
# TRAILHEAD

## A year in the northern wilderness

Joanne Ronan Moore

**Deneau & Greenberg**

**Canadian Cataloguing in Publication Data**
Moore, Joanne Ronan, 1952-
Nahanni trailhead

ISBN 0-88879-034-1

1. Moore, Joanne Ronan, 1952- 2. South Nahanni Valley,
N.W.T.—Description and travel. I. Title.

FC4191.4.M66          917.19'3043          C80-090072-3
F1060.92.M66

©Deneau and Greenberg Publishers Ltd. 1980
305 Metcalfe St., Ottawa, Ontario

To John
with love and deepest appreciation
for the hours and energy so
willingly contributed to this book

# Contents

# Acknowledgements

The very nature of Nahanni Trailhead made it necessary for John and me to consult with more individuals than I have space here to name. However, our friends, fellow staff members, the helpful store employees we sought assistance from and especially Mr. Wally Schaber of Black Feather Wilderness Adventures and Captain Ed Hartlin of the Royal Military College in Kingston should not go unthanked. Their interest and support fuelled our enthusiasm.

To those kindred spirits we met on the Nahanni who shared a campfire, tea or conversation with us, our warmest wishes. To Dwight Herbison, Pat Wood and the Sandes at B.C. Yukon, we extend our warmest appreciation.

To our sponsors, Dwight Rockwell and the Grumman Corporation, Splitkein Skis, Eureka/Camptrails and Hansen Mills, our thanks for their contributions.

To our families, who must have questioned our sanity at times, these words are too few, but John and I are grateful for their guidance and unwavering confidence in us. Without them it would have been a much tougher road.

And finally a very special thanks to Lynn Martin for her careful attention to the maps and to Jim Moore, whose strong belief in this book made it possible.

# Prologue

John and I were sitting next to a campfire when he proposed that we build a cabin in the wild and remote Nahanni Valley and live there for one year. His plan was contingent upon my accepting a second proposal — that I go there as his bride. I happily said yes to both.

We had been dating for almost two years and our mutual love for the outdoors was one of our strongest bonds. During many camping and canoeing weekends in southern Ontario, John had shared with me his fantasy of living in the Nahanni Valley and running the whitewater of the legendary South Nahanni River.

His dreams had been sparked by reading R.M. Patterson's *The Dangerous River* — the recollections of a life of trapping, prospecting and hair-raising adventure in the Nahanni Valley during the 1920s. After reading the book I shared his passion for this mysterious corner of Canada's northern wilderness, but not in my wildest dreams had I expected to be party to such a scheme.

The Nahanni Valley is in Canada's Northwest Territories, close to the border of the Yukon Territory and cut off from the outside world by several mountain ranges. Its treacherous "highway" is the South Nahanni River — as savage a waterway as any in North America — that carves its way through cliffs a thousand feet high and pours over the world-famous Virginia Falls (twice the height of Niagara).

The southern portion of the river was made a national park in 1972 and boasts some of the most magnificent and varied scenery on the continent, from the mountains with their free-roaming wildlife, to the hotsprings with their tropic-like vegetation. For camper, canoeist and naturalist alike, it is a wilderness paradise.

As enticing as its beauty is the valley's mythology and its cloudy history. Often called "Deadmen Valley" for the tragedies that have occurred there, it remained virtually sealed off and unexplored by white men until late in the nineteenth century. The *Nahani* and *Slave* tribes (Athabaskan Indians) are said to have moved into its lower reaches in the eighteenth century after being driven out of their hunting grounds on the

Liard River by the Cree. They lived a nomadic existence and left few traces of their presence. The name Nahanni is translated as "the people-over-there-far-away," which seems the perfect name for the valley they lived in.

Not until the Yukon gold rush did outsiders begin to penetrate the valley, seeking another route to the gold fields. Most of the fortune seekers travelled the Yukon River, but some are reported to have ventured up the Nahanni, hoping to cross the Continental Divide at the river's source and then raft down the Pelly River to the gold fields. When men disappeared in the valley, the Indians were blamed; little was known then about the natural hazards of the South Nahanni River. One infamous case of foul play added fuel to the speculation.

In the early 1900s Charlie and Willie McLeod ventured into the valley seeking placer gold. When they failed to return a search party was mounted, and in 1906 their remains were discovered — headless and tied to trees. Newspapers headlined the story, and thus the names Deadmen Valley, the Headless Range, and Murder Creek. Earlier rumours crystallized into printed stories of head-hunting Indians.

In subsequent years the Nahanni continued to attract a handful of adventurers, lured by the thought of gold and the much more tangible prospect of bringing out a fortune in furs. One of the most prominent of these men was R.M. Patterson, whose writings about his own experiences and those of the legendary Albert Faille (a man who spent most of his lifetime trapping in the valley) helped to dispel the horror stories.

Today the Nahanni is more and more the preserve of recreational adventurers and employees of mining companies. It remains as dangerous a land as ever, but the dangers are from accidents, exposure, or encounters with wild animals. Most of the substantiated deaths have occurred on the river, which shows no mercy to the careless or the unprepared.

When we began to make our plans John and I were aware of both the spectacular natural beauty of the valley and its hazards. Since we intended to build a cabin, we would not be in the relative safety of Nahanni National Park, but far upriver, near the junction of the South Nahanni and the Little Nahanni.

Our odyssey began that night, huddled around the campfire. We gave it a code name — Nahanni Trailhead — and began compiling a tentative list of supplies. It was the beginning of nine months of preparation: endless discussions about possible oversights, countless hours of research, continuous revision of our list and, finally, the biggest, maddest shopping spree you can imagine.

We were both teaching that year, in Kingston, Ontario, and every free minute was devoted to what became more and more like a military operation. Our supply list was separated into categories and expanded into the pages of what we called our Black Book (see appendix). We divided the duties according to our respective areas of expertise.

John was by far the more seasoned woodsman. He had progressed from summer camper and camp counsellor to leader of canoe and backpacking trips into Northern Ontario and Quebec while attending Queen's University in Kingston. He had also managed a camping goods store and helped plan large-scale trips into the north. This experience and the carpentry skills he'd learned from his father made him the natural choice to look after building equipment and camping supplies.

My love for outdoor sports was fuelled as a child but my training in wilderness camping was neither as formal nor as intense as John's. Not until my final years in the School of Physical and Health Education at Queen's and my meeting with John did I further my education in the area of canoeing and backpacking. It was my health background that was an asset, especially my work in fitness and nutrition programs. This prepared me for the supervision of food and first aid supplies.

To help us finance the trip, John, with his business background, assumed responsibility for writing letters to various companies that might act as our sponsors while I took to the sewing machine to make what I could in the way of camping gear and storage bags.

During the nine months of preparation, every minute not taken up with teaching duties was spent organizing ourselves. The list of supplies, once compiled and separated into categories was added to daily — we ended up with pages and pages of what we called our Black Book. When we felt our research was complete, we armed ourselves with every catalogue imaginable and set to the task of approximating the total weight and cost of each item. After much review, we arrived at a four thousand pound weight limit and spending allowances so stringent there was no chance to indulge of any of life's extravagances. We didn't mind, though if it meant we could make our dream come true.

The groundwork laid, what remained was the most time-consuming exercise of all — acquiring the goods we needed to be self-sufficient.

Shopping for supplies was an adventure in itself. A good number of the store employees we dealt with either didn't believe us, didn't understand, or thought us so mad they didn't really care. One we consulted on chainsaws listened with interest to us for quite sometime before his eyes brightened and he went bounding into the storeroom to retrieve "just the right machine for you." Minutes later he returned with a high-powered saw and fervently explained what a prize piece of equipment it was. We were grateful for his advice but sadly aware that he hadn't understood a word of what we'd said. Jutting out from the rear of the thing was an electrical fixture — he'd throw in an extension cord as an added plus.

Our parents soon realized their attics were about to be rid of second-hand tools and odds and ends for our house needs, and fellow workers and roommates were bombarded daily with questions that arose as we worked our way through the lists.

As our departure date neared, our apartments became so cluttered with boxes we could hardly move and our pocketbooks were emptied into a mutual account for our purchases. By May 1978, we had spent eight thousand dollars and another four thousand was set aside for travel to the north and plane flights into our site. Our plan and our outfit were shaping up.

After our wedding and a relaxing week in Bermuda, we headed north for our dream honeymoon, with half our gear in a U-Haul behind our rusty but faithful Volvo; the remainder was sent by CN Express. Ahead of us was a three-thousand-mile drive to Watson Lake in the Yukon. Then, Nahanni Trailhead.

What follows in the pages ahead is a journal of our wilderness year, compiled from diary notes written at the end of almost every day. The focus of our year was our cabin, which still stands on a heavily forested bank of the South Nahanni River, sixty miles above the western boundary of Nahanni National Park. It was from this trailhead that we based our wilderness wanderings over the course of four northern seasons. It is of our experiences during this twelve-month period, of our travels by canoe, foot, snowshoe and ski and of the isolated land we came to love, that I write.

I offer you my impressions and reflections of a year in Canada's Northwest. It was a first year of marriage, a year of true wilderness adventure, of personal successes and delightful surprises.

# Nahanni Trailhead Begins

A breathtaking scene unfolded before me — the awesome beauty of mile upon mile of snowclad mountains, some sloping gently skyward from the valley basin of lush green forest where twisted rivers ran, others rising almost vertically. Snow still capped each majestic peak, but on the mountain slopes the patchwork of forests, meadows, and rock ledges promised summer.

Through the small window of the Otter, I scanned the U-shaped valley, carved by a glacier centuries before. Like a giant bulldozer, the moving ice sheet had gouged out the valley, smoothing and deepening its sides. Where soil and debris had been carried along with the ice, new landforms had been created, among these a number of small lakes.

The wild country beneath me was vast, untouched. In spite of all our preparations and research its size and solitude awed me. What challenges were in store for John and me in this fabled valley? My emotions seesawed between excitement and apprehension.

John, seated in the rear of the plane amongst piles of food and equipment, was poring over our topographical maps.

Occasionally he would look up to study a land form, then try to locate it on the map.

I waved to attract his attention and mouthed the words, "Where are we?" Talk was impossible over the roar of the Otter's engine. John gathered the bundle of material in front of him and came to sit next to me. He pointed first to Watson Lake, Yukon, our point of departure, and then traced our route up the Hyland River, past the mining camp at Tungsten to the spot we were now flying over. He pointed out the mountains to our left and right — the Bologna and Ragged Ranges. Our pilot, Ray, was following a northeasterly course down the Bologna Creek Pass.

As we flew out the pass, John flashed a thumbs-up sign. I turned and craned my neck at the front window. Our trailhead was now only minutes away.

From my front seat perch, I spotted a ribbon of murky green water below, cutting its way through a wide valley bordered by craggy mountains.

*Loading the Otter at Watson Lake, Yukon*

Here, at last was the South Nahanni River itself — the source of our past dreams and the inspiration for our adventure.

Three miniscule dots of brilliant blue came into view — the Island Lakes, our landing spot. The lakes in Canada's Northwest Territories are so numerous that no accurate count exists. This anonymity and the rugged surroundings help preserve their unspoiled beauty. The Island Lakes are three such bodies of water, although busier than many because of their strategic location. They lie within hiking distance of the South Nahanni River and have become popular landing lakes for the local bush pilots. Canoeists, eager to run this renowned river, often begin their journey here, approximately sixty miles from the headwaters of the South Nahanni watershed.

John and I intended to set up camp on the bank of the river. Now, as we began our descent, we peered anxiously out of the window. We were searching for the path we had been told would lead us from the largest of the Island Lakes to the shore of the South Nahanni River. Landing at the path's opening onto the lake would spare us the arduous task of packing our gear through dense bush. Our first load alone weighed sixteen hundred pounds and there was another twenty-four hundred pounds still to come.

The Otter descended effortlessly, angling towards the surface of the sky blue water. At the instant before we swept over the treetops, I caught a final glimpse of the weathered peaks.

Swoosh! The floats made contact. Waves broke the still surface, the engine buzzed and we were jostled about as the plane slowed and bobbed gently up and down. I glanced at John, who shook his head. Neither of us had seen a break in the shoreline growth.

We taxied around the lake for a second look, but again our search proved fruitless.

After checking for landing sites, Ray nosed the Otter up to a steep grassy embankment. John climbed out, secured the plane to a nearby alder, and went to look for the elusive trail. I sat on one of the floats, scanning the lake's perimeter.

"Not a bad spot at all," I said, putting on a good front. The truth was, the lack of a good trail would mean a drastic change in plans.

The shoreline looked less inviting than from the air. There were few spots one could go ashore on foot and all were unsuitable for unloading a plane full of cargo. The north and south slopes were steep and covered with dwarf spruce, birch and alder. The ground bushes were so intertwined that progress through them would be difficult even without a load, and

*Our first look at the Nahanni River Valley*

the moss that supported the more fragile growth and gave the forest floor a matted look would be murderous to trudge through with heavy packs. At either end of the lake the ground levelled off but it was swampy. Good natural landing sites or unloading docks seemed nonexistent.

John returned some minutes later. "I saw three moose in the swamp just west of here," he told us. But he could find no trail.

Before boarding the plane in Watson Lake we had joked about attaching our own names to landmarks. "Big Island Lake" was the name given our landing lake, because it was the largest of the three and contained a small, centrally located island. We now had a name for the adjacent body of water — "Three Moose Lake." We might not be making progress with our unloading but we were settling in in other ways.

"There are lots of game trails around that we can use as paths," John said.

"Let's unload here then," I suggested. "It looks as good a place as any."

We piled things as best we could on the side of the hill. It was steep, and it became slippery as we trampled back and forth over the moss. As soon as the plane was empty Ray uncoiled the ropes and bade us farewell.

"Do you know how to set up that aerial?" he shouted, as he climbed aboard the Otter. We assured him we did.

"Make sure it's going east and west!"

We stood amongst our scattered pile of gear, shouted our thanks and goodbyes and waved him off.

Long after the drum of the Otter's engine had faded we remained motionless on the steep bank. After nine months of anticipation and diligent planning we had at last arrived at our trailhead. We had expected to feel euphoric; instead, we were confused and overwhelmed.

For a long while we gazed over the quiet surface of the lake and its backdrop of mountains.

"Its seems a little strange to really be here doesn't it?"

"Yep," John answered. "Mountains sure do look different on paper."

"It's so quiet too."

John seemed unwilling to carry on a conversation or make a move, so I left him to his study of the mountains and whatever thoughts he wasn't voicing. In three weeks of marriage I had learned that pushing him for his reaction to something before he was willing to offer it was pointless.

I sat down on a rocky ledge. Breakfast had been in the early hours, and now, engulfed by silence, I couldn't dismiss the groans from my stomach any longer. I laid bread, salami and cheese on my overturned pack and offered John a sandwich.

OUR LANDING SITE ON BIG ISLAND LAKE
HIKE ON FIRST DAY
PORTAGE ROUTE
ROUTE DOWN SNAKE CREEK

N

SOUTH NAHANNI RIVER

THROUGH FOREST TO
SOUTH NAHANNI RIVER

FROM THREE MOOSE LAKE

I smiled to myself, thinking about last night's conversation. We had been dining in one of Watson Lake's finest eating establishments, talking about our first night in the wilderness.

With the assurance (from a reliable source) that a path led from Big Island Lake to the South Nahanni River, we felt entitled to make elaborate plans. Our first evening in the bush was going to be a dandy! We were going to set up a camp akin to an army command post, with a well-rigged cache to store our food in, both tents securely pitched, a waterhole located, a well-built fire pit and handmade chairs set up, a tarp raised in case of foul weather — on and on the list went. We continued talking well into the night, and by the time we made our way back to the local campground we were dizzy with plans.

So much for good intentions, I thought, and John echoed me. "We're really in a bit of a mess," he said.

My temporary paralysis was fading and a full stomach made me optimistic.

"I think the first thing we should do is try to find the river."

John agreed, and we set out with day packs, field glasses, the gun, and some ammunition. We tried to travel in as straight a line as possible through the stunted forest. Game trails were numerous and weaved this way and that, crisscrossing each other at intervals. We followed one and then another, all the while checking our direction of travel with a compass.

Soon the face of the forest changed. Birch, poplar, and spruce loomed large and healthy, offering a screen from the blazing sun. We had crossed the line between an impoverished forest and one of stately, well-nourished trees.

We veered off the trail we had been on, because it kept following the contour of the lake. Redirecting ourselves south, we climbed a grade that led through a dense stand of timber and into a knee-deep network of low sprawling shrubs and thick spongy moss. We were halted at the edge of a steep cliff.

Below us lay a wide area of marsh and beyond it, to the south and southwest, rose heights of land similar to the one we were standing on. We had no choice but to ford the shallow marsh. We scrambled down the cliff, rolled up our pant legs, and put the odds and ends that hung loosely around our necks into the daypacks. John led the way across the marsh, using the scattered clumps of turf and grasses as stepping stones.

"I hope the South Nahanni is beyond this hill," he groaned, as the miniature island he was standing on gave way beneath his weight. Water oozed inside his boots but he kept going, because the longer he stood in one place the deeper he sank in mud. I wasn't allowing myself any rest between hummocks. I was sure the muddy bottom of the marsh was a haven for leeches.

We got small comfort when we reached the top of a tree-studded rise. We were no closer to the river. A stand of thick timber made visibility to the south poor, but we could see another height of land and decided to climb it.

At the top of the hill we stood absolutely still and listened.

"I hear it!" I whispered, and felt greatly relieved when John nodded agreement. The South Nahanni's voice was being carried on the wind towards us.

It was another hundred yards, through a screen of ragged spruce, to the edge of a hundred and fifty foot bluff. And there she was — a grey, silty mass of water, raging between her banks, with as many uprooted trees in her clutches as there were upright ones on the shore.

"We've come a long way to see this!" John exclaimed.

The current was incredibly swift and strong. Whole trees with their root systems intact rocked on the water; as many as five at one time stretched across her width. The South Nahanni was approaching high water — a seemingly irresistible force.

As happy as I was to be standing on the banks of the legendary river we'd come thousands of miles to live beside, our immediate dilemma remained. None of the terrain we'd covered was suitable for camping; it was only sparsely treed and virtually all swamp.

"I'm not convinced this little outing has been all that successful." I said cautiously. John agreed.

"You're right Jo. None of it suits our purposes. There's not much on that opposite shoreline either. We'll have to do more scouting, but right now we'd better get back to the lake." Storm clouds were moving in quickly.

We decided to try a different route back to our landing spot in the hope of finding a path.

To our good fortune, however meagre it was that day, we were able to ford the creek at a beaver dam. From there it was a climb up through more stunted forest, until the lake's most westerly point was in full view. To the east, less than a mile away, was our load of supplies, and in front of us, the first flat and dry spot we had set eyes on all day. What a welcome sight! We were two weary travellers.

The discussion of what next to do amounted to no more than "Camp here?" and "Yep!" We took one more look at the darkening sky and decided to ferry everything as quickly as we could.

Our eighteen foot aluminum canoe, with custom-built aluminum bathtub in tow, made moving the supplies easy, but loading and unloading them was a different matter. By the time we'd finished lugging everything to shelter beneath two big spruce trees, we were completely exhausted.

Tea. Its the drink of the north, they say, the cure of all cures when a day on the trail has taken its toll.

John and I needed the cure and now, with steaming mugs of sweetened Earl Grey, we slowly returned to life. The day's events had left us sorely tired. We were disappointed — we had expected so much and felt we had accomplished so little.

Small wonder though that we felt worn out and a bit deflated. For the past nine months our lives had been a whirlwind of teaching duties, organizing our trip, and, last but not least, wedding preparations. The fresh air and the difficulties of our first day combined to make this whole hectic year catch up with us at once.

But, with dinner bubbling on the open fire while we sipped our hot drinks, we began to recuperate quickly. Although camp was not the fancy arrangement we had intended, it was a warm glowing fire, comfortable ground to stretch out on, and shelter. As though in sympathy, the clouds had spared us a deluge, and we watched the sun dip behind the western mountains, casting evening shadows across the violet sky.

In the excitement of arriving we hadn't even thought of looking at our aerial photographs, purchased from the Department of Energy, Mines and Resources in Ottawa. We had spent countless hours studying these overlapping photos with a stereoscope, because they outlined the area we were flying into and had enabled us to choose our location sight unseen.

Examining them now, we saw that our route today had bypassed the most promising campsite. The only group of large trees lay south and east of our circular route.

"Tomorrow, let's canoe to the eastern end of the lake and follow the dense treeline to the river," John suggested. When we turned in we were eagerly looking forward to our second day.

I rolled out of my polarguard bag and sucked in a breath of cool mountain air. Yesterday's hill climbing exploits had left one or two joints in need of oiling, but nothing that a little more exercise and a warm sun could not remedy. The golden disc was topping the horizon, and I could feel the rays penetrating the light nylon of our tent.

A crackling fire was soon ablaze and the coffee water boiling, while scrambled eggs and oatmeal cooked in their pots. We sat on stumps, taking in the bleached blue sky, snow crusted peaks, and streams of sunlight shimmering off the dark greens of the forest. It was a fine morning!

When we shoved off into the bay, the lake was like a mirror. The dip of our paddles was the only sound as we crossed to the most easterly end and nosed the canoe up to a bank.

Last night's review of the aerial photos had made us both more confident, and we had agreed that if finding what we wanted meant combing every foot of our new home, so be it.

Shortly into our hike, we came upon a mountain stream swollen with spring runoff. We followed it until it fed into the creek we had forded the previous day. The water ran deeper here, and on the far side was a forest unlike any we had seen. Spruce, tall and stately, stood like pillars. This was a forest that spoke of growth and destruction over many decades. Shattered and twisted ruins — the result of lightning storms and high winds — lay half buried in a lush covering of ferns and feather moss.

"Incredible," I cried. "John, this is it!"

We knew from our photographs that this was the edge of the heavily forested area where the trees were big enough to provide logs for our cabin. According to the photos it was only about a mile to the South Nahanni River.

The game trails formed a labyrinth of well trodden paths, some two feet deep with pillows of moss banking their sides. The fragance of spruce boughs was strong and sweet, and the stand of timber so dense that its canopy of interlocking boughs allowed little sunlight to penetrate.

The path we were following met a game trail running beside a small stream. It was almost an expressway — a hardpacked, two-lane affair that looked recently used. We headed west on it, with the heavily treed area on our right and the channel of silty water on our left.

Not far from the intersection of the trails, we rounded a sharp corner. This bend in the trail had hidden from us a majestic spruce that towered many feet above its neighbouring trees. Its size and the umbrella effect of its lower branches created a large shaded area at the base of its trunk. The flat dry ground covered with a bed of needles was ample room for our four-man Eureka tent.

Water was plentiful; there was a snye (a narrow channel of water branching off from the main flow of the river) a few feet away, and firewood and kindling lay virtually everywhere in the form of deadfall. It was one of those natural tent sites waiting for a potential occupant to come along and claim it.

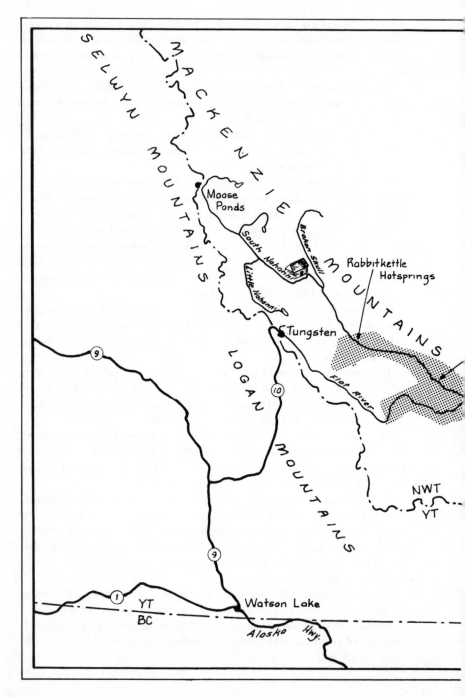

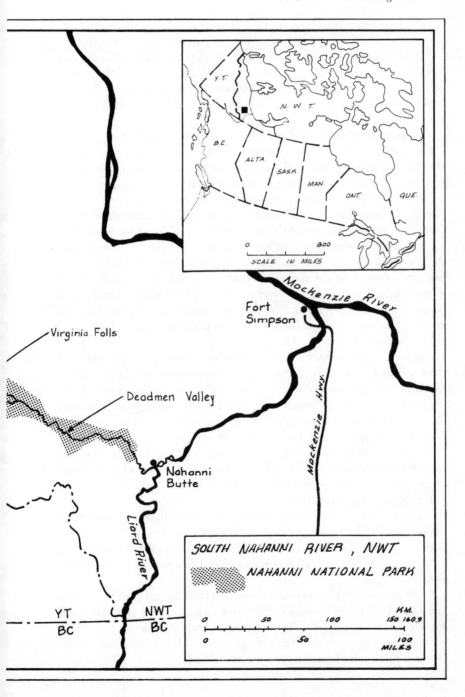

Virginia Falls

Deadmen Valley

Fort Simpson

Mackenzie River

Mackenzie Hwy.

Nahanni Butte

Liard River

YT
BC

NWT
BC

SOUTH NAHANNI RIVER , NWT

NAHANNI NATIONAL PARK

KM.
0        50        100    150 160.9

0              50              100
MILES

SCALE   IN   MILES
0        800

Y.T.

N. W. T.

B.C.

ALTA.

SASK.

MAN.

ONT.

QUE.

"What do you think of this spot Jo?" John stood studying the area from all angles; he had seen plenty of sites in his years of wilderness camping.

"There's water, firewood, sun, shade, wind protection," I began, but John's nod of agreement stopped me from going any further. We liked it.

Before committing ourselves, we decided to hike along beside the snye to what we hoped would be its convergence with the South Nahanni River.

The look of the forest caught my eye, and I stared about, trying to figure out why I felt so much more removed from civilization when walking through these woods than in the forests back home. The spruce trees, tall and straight, with wide boughs sweeping outwards from their thick trunks, towered above the rest of the forest. Beneath them were crooked poplars and thickets of high bush cranberries. The ground was a dense tangle of vines amongst the thick moss and pieces of decaying deadfall. It was the absence of human markings that made this forest different from the conservation areas we had frequently hiked through. There was no one here to manicure the growth and hold it in check. Even the the major game trail we were on was overgrown in sections. Apart from John, I wasn't apt to meet another human being, and this, coupled with the knowledge that several mountain ranges separated us from the nearest town, made me feel truly alone.

A short distance further we entered another clearing, one more perfect than the first. Four lofty spruce stood out prominently in a stand of smaller trees; they formed a rectangle, their upper boughs interlocking. No summer sun shone through and no ground bushes or plant life could eke out an existence at their feet. The ground at their base was firm and level. For the purpose we had in mind, it was grand.

The sound of rushing water was clearly audible. Heavy shoreline growth obstructed the view, but the dull roar and splashing voice could mean only one thing — the South Nahanni River.

We pushed our way through the thicket of alder. There was the tremendous flow of the river, behind it a magnificent panorama of mountains. By the time the alders sprang back, we knew this was more than a camping spot. Our cabin could command no better view.

"Let's check for the high water mark before we make any final decision," said John.

From previous experience in the woods of the Precambrian Shield, we knew that high water leaves a visible mark on large boulders, but no such rocks existed here. The piles of driftwood at the base of the alders convinced us we were on high enough ground. If the river rose to the clearing those piles would have been carried away.

"What are you thinking?" I asked John.

"This is the place. We can camp in the first clearing while we're getting the site ready."

Who could argue? The scenery was outstanding, the ground level and dry, and the trees ideal for building. The thick carpet of moss would provide the best natural chinking material, and there was plenty of firewood available. All the requirements for our first home were here — and in generous quantities. Our dream was taking shape.

We headed back to the campsite at Big Island Lake, full of ambition. With several hours of sunlight remaining we could begin to cut the portage trail necessary to move our supplies. The hundreds of pounds of equipment lying under the tarpaulin and the foodstuffs that would arrive in less than two weeks made up an outfit designed to meet all our needs for a year. We bounced along on the spongy carpet of moss, accompanied by the chirps and squeaks of startled deer mice.

As we closed up camp and loaded our canoe and packs, we realized the priceless value of our Black Book (see Appendix). It listed every item we owned, the code number of the box or bag it was in, and the weight of each parcel. On our first portage we would carry only the supplies needed for setting up a new camp: tent, sleeping bags, food for two weeks, cooking utensils, clothing, axes, saws, and various smaller essential items.

Our plan was to clear a swath out of the forest for about fifty yards, double back and portage our loads, then continue cutting.

John was ahead of me on the trail, nipping at the bases of the stunted trees and bushes with the whirling blade of the chainsaw while I followed with the axe, clearing away the brush and levelling strays he'd overlooked.

He had no trouble taking down large trees with the chainsaw, but in the tight clusters of alders there wasn't room to manoeuvre the blade safely. I chopped at them with the axe but couldn't take a good swing without getting caught up in the tangle of branches. After a round I was more than happy to take a break from axework and retrace my steps to retrieve the packs.

"Feel like a break after this haul?" John asked.

"Sure. But I'm so sore I may never get off the ground again!"

"Take as long as you want. I've got a minor adjustment to make on the saw."

"Problem?"

"A little one," John chuckled. "The chain's in backward."

We kept cutting until seven o'clock despite rain showers and the arrival of hordes of mosquitoes.

We packed enough equipment to set up camp, then waded through the icy water, paying little attention to the dark clouds rolling in. The tent would be pitched quickly, and we would be warm, dry, and full of food.

I learned one lesson from the day's labour that I won't soon forget. Never again would I hike along a previously cut trail without offering thanks to the blessed soul who toiled over its making.

# SNAKE CREEK

*June 5th*

Only one part of our portage route into camp posed a major problem — the creek crossing. It was one thing to wade empty handed through the numbing cold water and oozing mud bottom of this watercourse, but quite another to carry forty or more pounds on our backs at the same time.

Aside from the risk of soaking the contents of our packs there was the stove to consider.

It weighs two hundred and fifty pounds (with the fire brick lining removed), making it almost impossible to portage. We speculated that it could be rolled along the path without damaging its steel frame (or John, who would be doing the major job of rolling it), but somehow we would have to get it across the creek bed. After some deliberation we agreed to try our hand at constructing a simply designed boardwalk such as we had often used when cross-country skiing in a provincial park near home. A crude version of this bridging affair would be our means of conquering the single obstacle in our path.

The decision made, we lost no time this morning in closing up camp and heading to the creek with our axes and saw. Two of the largest spruce we could find on the creek's south bank were felled. John dropped the rod-straight trees so they landed in the shallows and I chopped off the branches. Our teeth chattering in unison, we waded through the cold water to position the logs as best we could.

We thought we were employing the genius of two master engineers when we decided to rest the tips of these spruce on a large, protruding clump of grass and mud. The butt end of each tree rested nicely on the bank of the creek and the entire length of this span of boardwalk was above water. We bravely walked out on it. Plop! The island collapsed and we were left standing in the water, dumbfounded, wondering who or what was to blame.

Somewhat dismayed, but not disheartened, we devised a second plan. Support cribs, that's what we needed!

Our design was simple. We would cut several large poles about four feet in length and build up cribs for the platform of logs to rest on. The logs would crisscross atop one another to form a hollow cube.

After a gruelling two hours our boardwalk reached the middle of the creek. We were uncertain how secure it was, and to lay the next span we would have to work in water over our waists. We began to question the whole idea.

We sat down on a weathered and sodden log, chins cupped in our hands, and looked drearily at our work. I was beginning to feel I was on a seesaw. One minute our plan looked feasible and the next it appeared foolhardy.

The cribs were made without nails because the much prized four-and six-inch spikes we had included in our outfit were in carefully rationed supply; they were intended for use in log cabin and cache construction only. We could lash the spruce poles together and make two larger and more stable cribs for this deep section of the creek, but we wondered whether we could then secure the whole thing to the soggy creek bottom. Aside from these questions about what hardware to use, there were the time and energy factors to consider.

After much head scratching and pacing the shoreline, we decided to portage one more full load of supplies from the lake, and then estimate how long it would take to transport everything overland. We would make the final decision about continuing our boardwalk after this trial run.

The forest was in shadow as we approached camp with our packs bulging. We were two wet and weary souls. The sky was a grey shroud of low cloud and heavy mist, and the cold dampness of the air did little to revive our failing spirits. I tried to cheer myself with thoughts of warm dry clothing and a seat by the fire, but as I moved along the trail, each step more of an effort than the last, I knew I craved a hot bath more than anything — an unattainable luxury.

With great sighs of relief we wrenched the canoe packs from our shoulders and flopped into the tent.

It had taken us four hours to carry a hundred and twenty pounds from the lake. Add to this the time it took to hike back to the cache and refill our packs — one trip required five or six hours. When we multiplied this by thirty-three — we calculated that our four thousand pounds of equipment would take thirty-three loads to transport — we knew we had to find another way of doing it.

I sat in my crude chair — an upturned stump with its surface levelled enough to make it somewhat comfortable — kneaded the bannock dough and watched John as he sawed a piece of deadfall. I was sure that he felt as I did, bone tired and hungry beyond description, but as long as there was work to be done he would carry on without a word of complaint. It was this quality that I admired in him most.

After our meal we consulted the aerial photographs once again. A faint line on one photo seemed to indicate an open water route extending from our aborted boardwalk to Three Moose Lake. One other important detail was visible. Along the length of the route were several arms of water flowing south. One of these narrow tributaries appeared to be not fifty yards from where we were camped.

We were up in a flash and bashing through the bush like a pair of wild boars. Only one thought raced through our minds: if the channel of water did exist and held enough water to float a loaded canoe, we had an alternative plan. The creek would no longer be an obstacle but a godsend.

The marshland was aglow with the radiant colours of a low sun peeping through the masses of grey and purple clouds. We stood on the outskirts of our home forest peering upwards at a sky that was turbulent and stormy overhead but clearing to the west. The distant mountains were brushed in shimmering, liquid gold light, and the cotton textured clouds were a translucent reflection of the sun. The effect was breathtaking.

But it was the water at our feet that held us spellbound. If it was this deep all the way to Three Moose Lake, we could avoid the overland haul.

The scraggy forms of black spruce and the grassy knolls that seemed to jut out from the shallow depths of the creek were silhouettes against the warm-coloured horizon when we turned for home. We picked our way through the brushwood and sidestepped the spruce boughs as we walked cautiously through the dimly lit forest. We spoke in hushed tones, for we were learning that to spot the nocturnal prowlers we had to tread lightly and quietly.

We stayed up later than usual around our campfire, watching the storm clouds move out to distant parts.

"What must it have been like to be an early explorer in the north?" I thought aloud.

"Pretty rough at times."

It's difficult to imagine the hardships endured by men like Alexander Mackenzie and George Simpson, whose expeditions in the eighteenth and nineteenth centuries took them through some of the most rugged and dangerous wilderness in Canada.

"Can you imagine standing on the shores of the Arctic Ocean as Mackenzie did in 1789 — without an aerial photograph in your hand?"

*June 7th*

We were relieved to see everything in place when we got back to Big Island Lake. The cartons and cotton sacks were as we had left them, bound in their tarpaulin and protected from the elements. From Big Island Lake we would portage our canoe and packs down to Three Moose Lake, about a quarter of a mile away, and begin our quest for a water route. Not until we were sure the waterway was navigable would we load the Grumman to the brim and begin relaying the outfit.

We knew the layout of the marsh we'd tramped through on our first day. The aerial photos, too, were a valuable reference, but we were wary of relying solely on these for direction. We couldn't assume that the topography was the same now as when the pictures were taken — in August of the late 1940s.

For one thing the water table in August has dropped considerably, sometimes to the point where narrow rivulets or shallow streams are running nothing but air. All the possible routes of a creek such as the one we were hoping to travel might not show on a photo taken at this time. Travelling in June, when the rivers, mountain streams and creeks are approaching high water, could work in our favour. With a greater flow we might have more options open to us — more chance of error too if we didn't keep a check on landmarks and our direction of travel.

Once out in the middle of Three Moose Lake it was plain to see why the prehistoric looking beasts responsible for its name enjoyed this dead still water. Moose-feed, primarily aquatic vegetation in the summer months, was abundant. Scraggy black spruce clothed in witches hair moss bordered the lake's marshy shoreline, and hummocks topped with wheat-coloured grass stuck up amongst the water lilies like miniature islands. Deadfall leaned against the trees at every conceivable angle. Along the muddy shore and in the shallows of this algae-bottomed lake were the sunken hoof prints of moose, elongated and sharp-toed.

We headed towards the beaver dam that blocked the mouth of the creek. Water seeped from one weak spot in the dam — a V-shaped crevice midway in the structure of interwoven branches. The concrete-hard filler of mud, grasses, and twigs that the beavers used to cement the dam together had given way here. What remained was a perfect niche into which we nosed the canoe.

I hopped out onto the dry platform and steadied the canoe, while John crawled over the thwarts. Together we hauled it, hand over hand, into the deeper water below.

The banks of the watercourse were barely wide enough for the canoe, leaving no room to paddle. Before we could figure out a method of propulsion the bow turned slightly to the left, sending the stern right and wedging us in. We teetered back and forth, slightly broadside to the current.

For the next two hours we used our paddles as poles to inch our way through the labyrinth of winding channels that we had already christened "Snake Creek."

By the time we reached a small pool, we thought the creek was a feasible route — certainly preferable to the portage — so we turned around and headed back for our supplies.

We slid the craft onto the crescent-shaped beach of Three Moose Lake, and slithered up and down the steep hill in our mud-covered boots to relay three hundred pounds of gear into the canoe.

We were returning to the canoe with the last of the boxes when swarms of mosquitoes attacked us. We began swatting at the air like two bewitched medicine men. Whatever alarm had been sounded to unearth these bloodthirsty pests had worked well. They were now about us in suffocating numbers.

John suggested a tactical retreat to the middle of the lake to escape the siege, and I was into the canoe with paddle poised before he even realized what had happened.

"That was a fancy bit of footwork," he said. I had leaped over the pile of boxes in the canoe with a fifty pound pack on my back.

"Let's get out of here!" I replied.

We'd been warned about the numbers and the fearlessness of the northern mosquitoes, and we knew all the yarns — insatiable maneaters it is said, capable of driving even the most stoic of men to breaking point.

On the water the air was mercifully clear and we ate lunch while keeping an eye out for game.

Midday is not the best time for observing wildlife, for the animals are starting their siesta. Early morning and later in the day are the times they usually feed and roam about. But on this afternoon we paddled right up to a feeding moose. This bulky mass of sleek shiny hair and gangly legs was either too dumbfounded to move, or too obstinate to care. His forlorn and preoccupied countenance masked his feelings either way. He buried his snout in the lake and came up chomping sedately on a water plant. Only when a collision was imminent did he move, bounding off towards the shore and the safety of the forest with an agility that astonished me.

When we finished eating we began our first trip through the marshland with a load.

We had to hoist the canoe over beaver dams, and when the channel narrowed we bullied our way forward using brute strength on the paddles. Whenever we found ourselves locked into corners or partially hung up on tangled shrubbery we had to work the canoe free.

Often a channel would suddenly branch off into several smaller snyes, and we would lose time trying to find the most navigable one. If the passageway we were in turned out to be a dead end we had to back the canoe out and try another.

In the shallow sections we had to grab handfuls of buckbrush and heave. We slithered forward over hummocks and half submerged brush. The only blessing was the absence of mosquitoes. The little monsters hadn't discovered us on the creek yet.

Finally the canoe caught a wisp of current and began to move downstream in the manner that it was intended to. We recognized a height of land to our left as the rise we had climbed down on our first day's hike. We knew then that the constricted waterway would soon feed into a larger pool, and from there it was only a matter of locating the arm of the creek that led closest to our camp. Where the line of tall dark forest tapered southwest towards the river, we would find John's yellow T-shirt, left as a marker the previous evening.

The day ended on a happy note. Although Snake Creek was troublesome in sections, it was navigable. As John so aptly put it, "Running a barging service may not be a joy but it sure beats portaging."

*June 10th*

With the preliminary questions answered, namely, where we are going to live and how we will move our supplies, we have established a work routine. There are many chores in need of attention. The cabin site is to be cleared of waterfront greenery and trees, a job that will take at least a week of solid work. A cache has to be built before our year's supply of food arrives, and this new shipment of goods has to be brought into camp via Snake Creek. What activity (or combination of activities) we undertake each day is decided after breakfast and depends more on the weather than any preference either of us might have. If dark clouds loom over the horizon when we arrive at the arm of Snake Creek, we return to camp and exchange packs and paddles for axes and saws.

No matter what we do, it is well past our regular city dinner hour before we return to camp. The sun has lost its warmth by this time but not its soft radiance, and we are assured of a couple of hours of light to relax by before turning in.

Today we made a run to the lake, bringing back over four hundred pounds of supplies. The water was high in the creek due to last night's heavy rain. This made paddling easier and cut the round trip from seven and a half to six hours.

We used the time we'd saved to build overselves a picnic table. We cut out four sections from a large spruce, stood them on end in a rectangle, then set two six-foot half rounds (logs cut in half lengthwise) on top. The flat side of the half round was the seat. The rounded underside we left rough except for the ends which were flattened so the seat would be level on its supports. The same method was used for the table top, with four half rounds. These were supported on two large spruce laid across the ends of the seats.

Now John is checking our inventory list while I enter my day's notes in the diary.

For me, dusk is one of the finest moments — when the blazing sun begins its descent and the last of its rays filter through the interlocking boughs of spruce. A branch snapping from somewhere deep in the forest marks the prowling of some four-legged visitor. The tree tops, aglow with the last of the warm light, buzz with the gruff voices of the grey jays and the high pitched chatter of the red squirrels.

These evenings in the wilderness are becoming a cherished part of my day, for despite our early rising and twelve hours of hard labour, I feel, not exhaustion, but contentment. I look forward to snuggling around the open fire next to John, enjoying a game of cribbage or reading.

Our library consists of over a hundred and fifty books and if weight had not been a factor we would have brought more. In the city, we snatch a minute here or there to work through a novel, but not so in our wilderness home. This past week I read John Dean's *Blind Ambition* and John Fowles' *The Magus* and am ready to begin a reread of our Sierra Club book on backpacking.

A whole new avenue of learning lies waiting in the forest as well. After just a week of referring to our Field Guide series on plant, animal and bird life, we find ourselves looking with sharpened interest at the world we live in. We didn't come to the valley as naturalists, but we intend to learn a great deal during our year here.

Many of our friends back home questioned our decision to spend such a long time alone, their concern being that too long a period of isolation might be a strain on our relationship. While a week is not time enough to judge one's performance by, I can't help but feel that we've been through more ups and downs in our first few days in the valley than would occur at home in a month. And we're adjusting well. Our mutual love for the outdoors and the shared dream of building our log home are very strong. Already we have faced enough frustrations and physical challenges to know that we can take them in our stride. Working together to build a home for ourselves is as thrilling as I had hoped it would be.

It's reassuring to look over at John, tired as he is after the day's trip up and down Snake Creek, and know that he is a true companion and friend. We will grow as individuals during our stay in the valley, and I have no doubts that we will grow closer together as well. In just a week, I feel I know and understand him better.

*June 11th*

For a long stay in the wilderness, a cache is as essential as a waterproof roof over one's head. Years ago, when the trappers and prospectors made the Nahanni Valley their home, the construction of a food cache headed the list of precautionary measures to safeguard their belongings. Without a cache, supplies are in constant danger of being damaged by the elements or, in the case of food, devoured by any animal with an appetite for the contents of your larder.

This sunlit morning, over our usual huge breakfast, we talked about building our cache. The design would be similar to the log framed structure we had read about in R.M. Patterson's *The Dangerous River.*

We needed first to find four healthy trees at right angles to one another. This initial step proved the most difficult. We scanned the forest for large spruce, but no arrangement of four satisfied the requirements. In the end, we settled for a slightly trapezoidal grouping of four poplars. While John was clearing the underbrush with an axe, I built a ladder so we could lop off the trees' branches.

Two floor supports of five-inch diameter poles, which an estimated fifty floor poles would rest on, were nailed to the corner posts at a height of thirteen feet. Each of the floor poles would extend some two feet beyond these support runners. This precaution, and the section of stovepipe we tacked around the trunk of each post, would, we hoped, keep scavenging animals from entering the cache.

We cut and trimmed an additional twelve posts to make a skeletal roof frame and side walls. Our plastic tarp fitted nicely over the superstructure; it was securely fastened on three sides and left to hook down onto nails on the fourth or entrance side.

The cache was now ready for storing our more perishable items. Batteries, film, and what we had in the way of bulk food were out of the equipment tent and up on the cache floor by nightfall.

*The food cache*

*June 12th*

Today we turned on our two-way radio for the first time, to contact the B.C.-Yukon Air Service. Our bumbling efforts to string the aerial had almost convinced us we'd thrown away a small fortune in the purchase of the machine. We were relieved when static and the garbled sound of voices issued from the speaker.

"What does the booklet say about talking into it?," John asked as we sat inside our equipment tent, trying to muster the courage to phone out.

"You say exactly what's written here. '86 Watson, this is XNL 999.' Push the button to talk and let it up to listen. Say 'Over' when you're finished speaking."

John rehearsed the lines a couple of times before he pushed the button.

"What do I do if someone else is on the line? Are they on the same frequency as we are?"

"Wait, I guess," I said, shrugging my shoulders. In a few minutes the voices faded.

"86 Watson. This is XNL 999. Over."

"999, this is 86 Watson. Go ahead. Over."

John flashed a look at me that said he didn't know what to do next.

"Go ahead," I urged.

"Hello, this is John Moore calling from the Island Lakes. Over."

"This is Ray Sande, John. How are you and Joanne making out?"

A smile spread over John's face and he began to relax.

"Fine, just fine."

"How did you get your supplies over that creek?"

"That's a long story. We're using the canoe to ferry the supplies into camp."

"I wondered about that when I flew out."

"We're ready for the rest of the stuff now."

"This is the date we agreed on," said Ray. "I've arranged for another pilot, Dave, to fly in. He should be at the lake by mid-morning."

John and I canoed up Snake Creek to meet the plane, blessing the favourable weather as we paddled along. Dave was on schedule. We watched from shore as the Beaver lit on the water and taxied towards us. We had cleared a space on the bank so Dave could nose the plane as close to land as possible. He tossed out two lines of rope and we secured them to nearby trees.

"It's comforting to see this stuff again," I said.

"It's quite a haul. How did you ever decide what to bring?"

"Most of it's food. I made up a master menu and then just ordered in bulk."

All three of us wanted to keep talking, but Dave had our second load to bring in.

"I'll see you in a few hours," he said.

The task ahead of us was an arduous one — putting the new supplies under the tarp, loading the perishables, paddling down the creek, and finally portaging the supplies into camp and the safety of the cache. But the thought of mail from home, which Dave would also deliver on the final run, was a great source of motivation.

At five o'clock the second load arrived and we were there to meet it. Dave stayed longer this time. He was anxious to learn about our first days in the valley. An avid outdoorsman, he questioned us on our plans for the year, nodding his head enthusiastically whenever we spoke of hiking in the mountains. Bush pilots, it seems, have the rare opportunity to witness wildlife encounters from their aerial vantage point. Dave told us of seeing a moose and a black bear locked in a death grip on a mountain meadow not far from our location.

"It would be wonderful to live and work here for a few years," I said.

"You know what they say — you get hooked on this country. You may leave but you'll always come back!" On that note our friendly pilot left us.

*June 14th*

It was the end of a particularly humid day; not a whisper of a breeze helped to stave off the energy draining closeness of the air. I was preparing dinner while John was at the cache.

Suddenly I heard a thunderous crack followed by a confusion of noise. Many times over the previous days I had felt my spine tingle on hearing the creak, then the moan, and finally the thud of a falling tree. But this sound was that of many falling trees, and a spasm of fear shook me — it came from the direction of the cache.

"John is underneath the cache!" I cried aloud and raced down the path.

I arrived at the cache breathless and numb with shock. John stood there — unharmed, thank god — but he said nothing to me, for he was as shocked as I at the debacle that lay before us. The entire floor of the cache had collapsed. Our year's supply of food lay in heaps on the ground and it was impossible to tell the extent of the damage. The tops of the margarine, jam and oil containers had flown off in the fall, and the contents of each now poured out in steady, multicoloured streams.

A twenty pound box of spaghetti had burst open, and the long noodles lay strewn amongst jars and tins. The only sound came from bags of salt, rice, sugar and oatmeal as the contents poured out onto the grass. To add insult to injury, six plastic pails of honey had cracked open, and the golden liquid now destroyed all that it touched.

We quickly collected what we could, in an effort to prevent further spoilage. John picked up the shattered bags and placed them in an upright position, clear of the other food and poles; I did the same with the jars of honey. Miraculously no further breakage had occurred.

We spoke for the first time since my arrival at the scene, and John explained what had happened. He was under the cache with a handful of brush when he heard a creak. He stepped back to eye the structure and, in an instant, the floor poles tumbled to the ground.

Now we were faced with the task of reorganizing our food supplies and rebuilding the cache before darkness fell. The rear cross support, holding up one end of the floor poles, had given way. Under the weight of the supplies, the six-inch spikes had popped, and the wire that was twisted around each post had snapped from the sudden stress. In rebuilding the structure we would have to strengthen the connection between all the posts and the floor supports.

John returned to camp for axes, hammer and nails while I tallied up the damage and tried to restore order to the rubble at my feet. I called to John to bring with him all the green garbage bags he could find; they would have to be used as storage bags now, because most of the cardboard boxes were smashed.

It took four hours of non-stop work to pack and label the food and rebuild the cache. The supports, which had been nailed and wired to the posts, were notched to fit more snugly, renailed, and then lashed with strong nylon cord. When this was done the floor poles were carefully set into place.

There was little spirit left in us as we sat on nearby stumps and tended to the fire of garbage smouldering at our feet. I felt only a dull ache through every part of me.

By sheer luck John was unhurt, and our pantry, while slightly modified, is nearly intact. Sweeteners will now have to be carefully rationed, but we are fortunate — there was no major loss of basic foodstuffs. It was the knowledge that we had not been more painstaking in building that troubled us. We vowed that such carelessness would not happen again.

*June 15th*

Each day of clearing our waterfront produces remarkable results. The view alone makes our choice of this cabin site seem perfect. With a hundred and twenty-five feet of clear frontage, we have a magnificent panorama of mountains.

At the foot of our clearing is a stony bar, partially submerged in water. The rocks are smooth and regular, like a cobblestone street, each pounded and moulded in its place by the force of the river. Skeletons of trees that have been carried from upriver are washed up on the bar, and a handful of bushes grows in the shallows.

Directly opposite the clearing is a high cutbank with a quarter-mile long sheer face. The eastern half is dotted with dwarf timber, but the western slope is eroding before our eyes. We have seen several large boulders dislodge and tumble into the South Nahanni, carrying with them fragments of the cliff and loose gravel. The swift and unrelenting current of the river eats away at the bottom half of the slope, until no support remains and the upper half collapses.

Beyond the cutbank rise mountain pinnacles crowned in white. The snow crystals glisten under the sheen of the sun and vast sheets of ice fill rocky crevices.

One mountain in particular has caught our eye, and we have named it "Snow White." It is one of those mountains that stands out amongst a range, that you can look at often, admiring its grandeur and absorbing some of its serenity.

To its right are "The Three Bears." They do not climb to the heavens like Snow White (I estimate their height to be seven thousand feet), but are rounded and cloaked in green and brown. Until our home is built we can only glass these mountains from the clearing, but already we are planning to explore their every nook and cranny, and by naming them we have laid claim to the horizon.

A short distance downriver from the clearing, the South Nahanni's surging flow splits around one of the many islands in this section of the river. Like the shoreline cutbanks, the extremities of these islands are under pressure from the constant impact of the river's current. They are broken down, carried by the current and later deposited elsewhere.

The mountains to which the river flows are the Mackenzies, a different cut and fold from those opposite our cabin. We don't know these austere elevations as we do the peaks of the Ragged Range, for they are miles away on the eastern horizon, but in their foreground stands a mountain of rustic tones and aged beauty that stirs our hearts. It looks like the grandfather of them all with its multicarved ledges that speak of many storms. It has not surrendered to the wind, rain, and snow that has carved out the hollow crevices in its sides. It stands rooted and strong, with the countenance of a giant. Under the amber light of the setting sun its earth tones deepen, and its jagged edges become a fiery orange. We call this distant peak "Big Red."

# Building the Cabin

In the early 1900s, the Northwest was thought to be made of solid gold. Gold rush fever set many dreams in motion, and men from across the continent came to battle this unmapped wilderness and unearth its treasure. The Nahanni Valley, for a time, had its share of prospectors and trappers, but stories of bizarre tragedy began to filter out of the valley and were picked up by the press.

Newspaper accounts in 1906 described the mysterious deaths of two brothers, Charlie and Willie McLeod. The men were found at the mouth of a creek in what is known today as Deadmen Valley, tied to trees with their heads missing. Other, less dramatic reports, of men presumed dead because they had disappeared in this little know land, fed the growing legend that there were wild men in the mountains of the Nahanni — head-hunting Indians it was rumoured — guarding vast quantities of gold. It was said that no man would return from his quest for the Valley's riches. Interest in the Nahanni slackened, amid an atmosphere of fear and superstition.

Still, as R.M. Patterson relates in *The Dangerous River*, there were men such as himself and his partner Gordon Matthews, who, later in the 1900s, defied the legends. Their adventures now have a place in the recorded history of this region of the North.

These were busy men, seeking their fortunes in furs and placer gold. Their winter cabins were hastily constructed and often deteriorated within a year or two. Comfort and long-term durability were minor considerations, because after they'd worked out an area, the inhabitants were ready to move on.

John and I were staying in the valley for only one year and we could have built our cabin with a similar philosophy in mind. But we had other plans, best addressed by explaining how we got permission to build in this isolated part of the North.

The lure of northern Canada attracts many people, but it is a misconception to think that anyone can choose a plot of land in this vastly un-populated area and construct a cabin there. All of the North is Crown land, administered by the federal government through the Department of Indian and Northern Affairs, and its use is carefully controlled.

John and I were told about a young man who built his wilderness re-treat without permission, and after repeated warnings to leave, returned home one night to find his cabin burned to the ground. It was presumed that the officials took the matter into their own hands.

It took no more to persuade us to decide on a different approach.

Initial inquiries, in September of 1977, led us to the Federal Lands Office in Yellowknife, Northwest Territories. We filed two lease applica-tions but received a negative reply in early December. We were told that new regulations had been in effect since 1975 limiting land leasing to de-signated subdivisions such as Yellowknife. Their purpose was to conserve waterfront development and control haphazard programs in the North.

Fortunately, a very helpful officer (then supervisor of the Federal Lands Office) suggested that, given our intended length of stay, we apply for a Land Use Permit. Such permits are used extensively throughout the North by timber and mineral exploration companies.

Our application was in the mail shortly before Christmas. It described the activities we hoped to undertake in the Valley and our plans to care for the environment. We outlined the dimensions of our proposed cabin, as the application requested, and stated our intention that it should stand for several years.

Canoeists who travel the South Nahanni River from its source (refer-red to locally as the Moose Ponds) or choose the Little Nahanni as an ac-cess route, must negotiate some sixty miles of rock strewn whitewater. Such a stretch of rapids can damage both equipment and people, and we wanted the cabin to house enough first aid supplies to serve as a vital way station.

We received the permit in January of 1978 — a quick reply indeed. I have always suspected that the officials decided a cabin in the area would be a sound investment and that our plans to build one earned us the quick approval. The cost of our hectare of land for one year? A mere twenty dollars.

Not being experts, we researched and collected information on trap-pers' cabins. These are quite small, because more often than not a trap-per's shelter houses a single occupant and he may have a second or third such station along the route of his trapline. Their average size is about ten feet square.

Given that our cabin was to serve as a permanent winter shelter for two, and that we had much more equipment than the average trapper, we drew up plans for a larger layout — fifteen by twenty-one feet. The rear wall, measuring twenty-one feet across, would be split into three seven-foot sections with the centre one jutting out to form a seven-foot square woodshed. This would solve the problem of working with long logs, which are difficult to find and would be cumbersome for the two of us to set into place. There would be a window in each side wall and one on either side of the front door, keeping the principle in mind that the more breaks we had in the long walls the greater the number of logs needed, but the shorter their lengths.

With the blueprint of the cabin complete, we took to educating ourselves in the ways and means of building a home. I, who had no building experience whatsoever, enrolled in a carpenter's course to acquaint myself with basic tools, and particularly to acquire some practical experience in using power tools. First, I had to overcome a basic fear of the chainsaw, for it would be our right arm in building the cabin.

John, who had learned rough carpentry skills from his father, was better prepared.

We both enrolled in a practical course on building with logs, given by a friend of ours, Chris Harris. He explained the round notch method of log construction, showed us how to fell trees safely, and gave us a realistic conception of how long it would take to build a cabin. We tried our hand at cutting notches and building up the walls of a log structure and after the weekend knew how to use and maintain our saws.

Next we read all the available books on the construction of log homes. These included Allan Mackie's series of books on log cabin construction, *Hand Hewn* by William Leitch, and a book published by the University of Alaska.

We figured out the exact quantities of spikes, roofing nails and tarpaper we would need. The dimensions of the windows and door were determined in advance, because wherever possible, as in the case of sill boards and plexiglass window panes, the materials were pre-cut and packed for transportation.

With all this buying and prepacking going on during the preparation months, our apartments soon came to resemble warehouses. There was little room left for us amidst cartons of food, bags of clothing and personal gear, boxes of first aid supplies, recreational equipment and containers filled with our endless list of necessary items.

Everyone stopping in for a visit eyed this assortment of goodies and either shook their heads in dismay or questioned us on our reasons for including one thing or another. Apart from the pleasure of talking with friends about our plans, these discussions on inventory helped us double-check the outfit and reevaluate our decisions on including certain items.

Our respective roommates were not only tolerant and supportive but, like our families, were involved from the start — offering suggestions and advice.

*June 19th*

One thing can be said for rising to a day when the air is brisk and the sky overhead is layered with foreboding clouds — you don't waste too much time getting underway. When I stuck my nose out of the mosquito netting to check on the day's weather, I was met with a blast of cold wind. Without even consulting the thermometer, I donned heavy wool socks and long work pants, grabbed a handful of sweaters, and squirmed into them as quickly as possible.

It was my turn to be the early riser. While I started the coffee pot brewing and began breakfast, John caught a few extra winks. When he scrambled out of the tent some fifteen minutes later, he huddled close to the open flames, and there we both remained until the last of the cheese omelette and pancakes had disappeared.

Dishes were cleared from the kitchen table and washed up in record time. Clothing, food, and equipment not needed for the day were stored in our second tent. Carrying tools and a light lunch, we walked down the path to the building site.

It is always exciting to enter the clearing in the morning and see the previous day's accomplishments. Except for short excursions during our lunch break or after dinner, we spend entire days there now. The brush piles in the southeast and southwest corners are all that remain of the heavy undergrowth that once blocked our view of the river and the mountains beyond. Unwanted stands of poplar have been removed and today we began cutting and stacking building logs — the final stage of site preparation.

It was ideal weather for working, because the colder air kept most of the mosquitoes away. Felling the large trees and dragging them off to the corners of the clearing, where they are stacked to dry, was sweaty work. We didn't need the sun to keep us warm, because once we started work the chilliness of the air went unnoticed.

Once a tree is down, we lop the limbs off with the axe. Then, using a double-handled drawknife, we lift a portion of the bark up, enough so that we can grab onto the stripped piece with our hand and pull the thick covering away. The bark peels off easily because the trees are dripping with sap.

From start to finish, it takes about thirty minutes to fell, delimb, debark, and stack a tree. We tried several poplar and white spruce before deciding that spruce was the better tree for building purposes — straighter and of uniform diameter. Debarked they are flawless.

At the end of a round of cutting, we record the length of a log on its butt end with a red lumber crayon and pile the cleaned logs on platforms of three cross pieces. Stacking them in this manner allows air to circulate around the logs. This speeds up the drying process and makes warpage less likely.

At the end of the day we had twelve logs ready to be notched and positioned into place. Of this tally, one is a floor log which was split down its length to make two half rounds. John had to use a chainsaw for this job.

I was thankful we had the power saws with us as I watched him grind through all sixteen feet of the ten-inch diameter log. He was straining every muscle to gain an inch of cut. Earlier in the day, when I had first unpacked my chainsaw, I had doubts about starting it up. The same fears that had plagued me when we bought the machines surfaced again. But I realized that certain jobs, like splitting logs, would be nearly impossible for us with only a handsaw.

Bringing chainsaws into the wilderness was one of our most difficult decisions. They are dangerous unless used very carefully, and we were worried about the effect of their noise on the wildlife. But there seemed to be no alternative. It would take twice as long to build a cabin without them.

We purchased one small and one heavy duty Homelite reluctantly and promised ourselves to use them only for the most time-consuming jobs — felling trees, slicing logs in half and notching.

I didn't realize how silent our world was until the saw was turned off this afternoon. Our own reaction to its loud ugly whine made us wonder how the animals were handling all the racket. As if in answer to our question, a cow moose came wandering into the clearing only minutes after the motor was cut. If she was as shocked to see us as she appeared, she need not have worried. When we came to our senses, we felt only stunned admiration for the beast.

Before making our way back to camp today, we drew up a list of the logs required to build the cabin, in order to keep track of our daily progress.

| Quantity | Size | Use |
|----------|------|-----|
| 4 | 25 ft | base and top (plate) logs |
| 16 | 18 | side walls |
| 15 | 16 | floor |
| 12 | 11 | front walls |
| 50 | 10 | back walls and woodshed |
| 20 | 16 | rafters |
| 250 | 12 | roof poles |

Had we had the time to cut all these logs in advance, we would have done so, for a log left to dry out for several months becomes lighter. This is not the sole reason for allowing downed timber to season, but it is an important consideration, especially if one or two people plan to build a home by themselves.

Building with seasoned timber makes more sense from a structural point of view as well. There is less settling when dried logs are used, because most of the log shrinkage has occurred before putting up the walls.

We are doing the next best thing to precutting and seasoning our logs — cutting the longest ones first. This includes the plate logs and all those needed for above the windows. When the time comes to lift and notch these at a height above our shoulders, we hope they will be sufficiently dried out to make the job easier.

*June 21st*

The day had been sunny and warm, but as the sun fell away to the west the chill of the evening air settled on the clearing. We pulled on our oiled wool sweaters and inched closer to the brushfire.

We had set a ten-foot high dome of alder and willow branches ablaze a few hours earlier and it was still burning hot. Each time we stirred the smouldering embers, an untouched limb or piece of dry bark would ignite into flame. We wouldn't call it a day until the last of the pile was thoroughly burned.

At midnight the sun set. The mountains were just an outline against the smoky blue sky, and we could no longer make out the details of the outcroppings of rock or the undulating lines that marked where the timbered valleys fanned out on the mountain slopes. The horizon was a grey, towering form with jagged lines.

"We'll have to stay up and watch the sun rise. Should be in an hour or so. Can you stay awake, Jo?"

I stirred the outer edges of the fire with my shovel, looking for live coals.

I was sleepy, but this was a special evening. We were celebrating the summer equinox and the eve of our cabin building days.

"I'll stay if we can fix ourselves a hot drink. I'm stiff with cold."

We waited until the last of the green timber had turned to ash then doused the blackened area on the rocky beach with buckets of water. The inner core of the scorching pit hissed and smoked. When it was safe to leave the sodden charcoal pieces unattended, we began to collect the gear.

To the southeast a golden halo was stretching out across the sky, an arc of light that illuminated the topmost contours of Big Red and the distant buttresses of the Mackenzie Mountains. The sun was beginning its ascent already, only an hour after dropping out of sight.

The forest was strangely quiet in the semi-darkness as we made our way along the path towards camp. The first beams of light danced over the faint impressions of animal tracks left in the soft earth. Rabbits and the neighbourhood red squirrels had been down the path recently, but there were no larger prints. Just this afternoon, we had caught a glimpse of what appeared to be a weasel slinking through the undergrowth. The meeting was so brief that neither of us could determine the animal's size or colouring. We could only hope that our visitor would return.

*June 22nd*

No matter how much one prepares for a task, the initial hurdle is perhaps the most trying and often not the most effectively handled.

While clearing the timber from the cabin site, we had selected and left standing two of the largest spruce in the forest. They stood about fifty feet high and well over eighteen inches in diameter — ideal for our base logs. Now we were ready to fell one of them and I was apprehensive.

"We want this one to fall to the west." John said.

I nodded and took my place next to this imposing spruce so I could alert John if any problems developed while he cut out a V-notch in the trunk about one and a a half feet from the base. Then he sank the spinning blade in at an angle on the opposite side. The cut was deep enough to force the tree to lean in the desired direction, but it still left two inches of the trunk intact. This is called a "hinge."

I was watching the topmost branches for signs of movement, and when the tree began to waver I screamed at John to get a safe distance away.

Despite his careful efforts, the tree thundered to the ground far from the mark we had chosen.

"Did you see that," John shouted, "the thing fell sideways!"

"Maybe this tree is warped or the wind caught it."

Whatever the reason for its wilfulness we were glad it had fallen easily. I measured off twenty-five feet while John started delimbing, then followed behind him and stripped the tree clean of its outer layer. We ran into difficulty when we tried to roll the immense log over to debark its underside. Several limbs had snapped off halfway and driven themselves into the ground. We used the butt end of a large spruce as the fulcrum and a long pole as a makeshift lever. John applied his full 190 pounds to the pole end, raising the log and the troublesome limbs. I sawed them off and we finished debarking the tree.

Next, we had to move the log into position. After successive failures with the block and tackle (the log would travel all of two feet and then dig its front end into the soft earth) we tried placing log runners beneath it. While John levered up one end at a time, I slipped the poles into position. After a breather we tried to move the tree.

"You watch the back end Jo. I'll direct the front. Give 'er a good shove! That's it."

The log promptly fell off its runners, and for a moment we began a Laurel and Hardy routine, John tugging his end one way while I pulled in the opposite direction.

"Jo do you know where we're going with this log?"

"Nope".

"Well I was following you!" His voice had an edge to it.

"Well maybe you were, but I wasn't going anywhere in particular."

"Let's sit down. I need a few minutes to clear my head."

We tried again after a rest. The runners were repositioned and the log rolled into place.

Once the first log was positioned and pegged to the ground to hold it securely, we devised an improved scheme to drop the second tree. John tossed a hundred-foot length of rope with a weight at one end into the crook of an upper bough, then walked a distance from the tree in the direction we wanted it to fall. He kept a firm grip on the rope while I cut out the V-notch. Before I began the second cut, he ran the rope around a nearby tree so he could stand a safer distance away but still have a free end of rope in his grasp. He kept the rope taut as I sank the sawblade deep into the spruce's core.

When I heard the hinge crack, I jumped free of the path of descent and down the tree came, with a resounding crash and a vibration that shook the ground beneath us. The spruce fell in the exact spot we wanted.

Everything worked better the second time. We soon had the second log aligned with the first, fifteen feet from it. The distance between the opposite corners of the two logs had to measure twenty-five feet, nine and a half inches to ensure a perfect right angle at each corner. We shifted each log until the measurement was accurate, then secured each one with heavy pegs.

The ground beneath the two was level enough that no major excavation was needed, but we dug shallow trenches under the wider butt ends to make the twenty-five-foot length horizontal. A carpenter's level verified this.

A solid foundation of cement is often used to prevent rapid deterioration of the underside of cabin base logs, but the silty soil on which the logs were resting provided enough protection from moisture damage. Trappers often set their logs in a trench of sand, which is a superb drainage material.

By early evening the side base logs were set into place, using a round notch method. We used handmade "log dogs" to hold the eighteen-foot lengths steady while we transferred onto their ends the dimensions of the base logs they would rest on. We could have used the log-gripping device made of steel with two bent and pointed ends, but our sturdy poles with spikes driven into each end worked well (and didn't cost us a penny). One end was hammered into the log to be fitted, the other into the placed log (in this case the base logs) that ran at right angles to it.

I didn't have the energy to even look at another log by the time we completed this stage. While we cleaned up wood chips and sawdust, I circled the area squared off by the four logs.

"Just think, in a few weeks we'll have the walls up! I wonder what the cabin will look like finished?" It was exciting to think about a floor plan and the kinds of furniture we would make.

We have a floor to lay in first though, a luxury that most of the old-timers did without. At this early stage of construction these trappers and prospectors would take shovel in hand and dig out about two feet of soil. The clay would be left to harden as flooring. The earth gave off enough heat to keep their toes from freezing and that was their main concern.

Some stories we've read describe a ground cover of poles, laid side by side. Although a step above a dirt floor, I think this type of flooring would leave a little to be desired. Unless the seam between each log was packed with enough earth to smooth the top surface, the finished product would give the feeling of walking on rollers.

We have a more refined plan in mind, and before leaving the site we did the preliminary groundwork to carry it out. We ran a string around the inside faces of the four logs that now formed a fifteen-by-twenty-one-foot rectangle. This was attached at each corner with nails and adjusted accordingly when we checked the line with our level. This marking is to be the bottom border of a shelf. Our floor boards, half round logs set flat up, will be notched on either end to sit on this shelf.

*June 28th*
There is only one prerequisite to enjoying a Yukon breakfast — an incredibly ravenous appetite! This morning I came to the table with a craving and capacity that astonished me. I put away two helpings of pancakes dripping in butter and maple syrup, topped with fried eggs and slabs of crispy bacon.

"Are you planning to set all the walls of the cabin in place today Jo? I've never seen you eat so much."

"It must be the fresh eggs and meat. I didn't realize how much I missed them."

We owed this feast to the generousity of two visitors, the Nahanni district geologist, Chris, and his pilot, Ian. The lime green helicopter bearing this amiable pair had dropped out of the blue while we were dragging a downed timber into the clearing some days before.

It had been more than two weeks since we had seen Dave, the pilot who brought in the remainder of our supplies, and we didn't expect any more visitors until mid-July, when the canoeists begin running the river. We were ecstatic when the chopper circled overhead and slowly dropped in altitude.

It came to rest right in the middle of the clearing. The whirling blades barely missed the poplar branches in front of us, and the loud buzz of the engine echoed through the stands of forest.

As we waited for our guests to disembark we became inexplicably nervous. John expressed a concern that maybe we had done something wrong and these men were coming to evict us. It was the one time I wished he had left his feelings unspoken. Now I was wondering what had brought them here.

Our welcome suggested the slightly abnormal behavior of two recluses. Later I had to laugh at how incoherent and sheepish we must have seemed. Our tongues were tied in knots. Not a word we said in the first few minutes came out naturally. We answered most of Chris and Ian's questions with short, static replies or long awkward pauses.

No sooner had we relaxed and gotten to know something about our visitors than it was time for them to leave. There were some mining camps in the area that Chris still had to visit before dinner. We were as sorry to see the helicopter lift off as we had been apprehensive about its arrival.

It was not until the next day that we fully understood the significance of

*Joanne cooking breakfast*

*Trimming up a floor board*

our conversation with these men. Chris had questioned us thoroughly on our food supplies when we showed him the cache, and he expressed an interest in our portable refrigerator — a grub box half submerged in the river.

We were on an afternoon hike when the helicopter returned. When we walked into the clearing later that day, we were dumbstruck. They had left us a box containing some needed chain oil, lettuce, tomatoes, bacon, two dozen eggs, a case of soft drinks, boxes of chocolate covered raisins and peanuts, and cans of shrimp and asparagus.

The incident illustrated something more to us than the generosity of these men. Having only read about "northern hospitality" we were not sure what made it unique. Now we knew. Chris and Ian's gesture explained to us something of the ways and the extent to which people of the north respond to one another's needs. The rugged environment and the distance between friends encourages a very special kind of sharing.

Breakfast done, we settled back into our easy chairs for a spell.

"I'm sure I couldn't eat another thing." John groaned.

"I couldn't either, but I'm fuelled enough to lay the last of those floor logs. Only four more to go!"

Cutting and fitting the boards into place was backbreaking work, but the nearly completed floor already gave the structure a look of permanence. The floorboards were cut from the largest spruce trees we could find. John peeled the bark off a sixteen-foot section and sawed the log into two equal halves. The neater and staighter his cut, the easier my job was.

I cut a notch at each end (on the rounded underside) so the logs would sit evenly on their supporting shelf. Once a floorboard was placed, I used our scribers to measure the greatest distance between the two boards sitting side by side, and then I trimmed the edges so the two would fit snugly together. Finally, using an adze (a tool much like an axe except that its blade is turned up in a slight curve and set at right angles to the handle) I made the floor surface level. To give the boards some support in the midsection, I took several small logs and wedged them in between the ground and the rounded underside of the log. Shavings, woodscraps, more earth, and strips of bark were shovelled underneath for insulation purposes. This done, the next log was heaved into position.

John had already prepared enough logs to complete the main cabin flooring. While I finished notching and fitting these, he started cutting logs for the floor of the woodshed, using the same technique.

The woodshed base logs were attached to the rear wall of the cabin, using a mortise and tenon joint. The ends of two nine-foot logs were cut down to a square tongue to fit precisely into two holes cut in the back base log. The tenon part of the joint was a six-inch spike, nailed through the base log and tongue to hold the joint firmly.

By early evening the floor of the cabin was complete. This entitled us to a bit of a celebration. We, the valley's two local inhabitants, held our first dance.

We performed reels and jigs, polka steps and waltzes, twists, turns, shuffles, and other moves we dreamed up as we danced on. It was an indiscriminate mixture of Arthur Murray and Saturday Night Fever, with no audience but the animals. Visitors, if they had dared come close, would surely have thought us mad.

### June 29th

After lunch we gathered together tents, clothing, food, kitchenware and all the odds and ends we owned and moved to the cabin site. It took twenty-one trips each to shift our provisions to our new location, but we didn't look upon the afternoon's activity as work. It was more like moving to a better house across the street. One tends to ignore the time and effort involved if there are benefits to be gained. In our case, there is no question about where we prefer to be. We felt confined in the heavily wooded area of our first camp. At the building site there is a feeling of spaciousness and brightness and an unobstructed view of the mountainous countryside. A light breeze that blows in off the river keeps the insect population down to a bearable level. The time for visiting canoeists is drawing near too, and we are more likely to meet people in an open spot overlooking the river.

We have enough land cleared to accommodate several tents, so canoeists passing through can stay on for a day or two if they wish.

Our growing collection of custom-made furniture is another sign of settling in. Our easy chairs (two poles driven into the ground at an angle function as chairbacks and a much larger log forms the seat) fit the contours of our bodies like few store-bought products can. The top surface of each seat log was smoothed with the adze and a shallow depression rounded out with the axe so our rumps fit snugly. They are a joy to rest in after the long hours of stooping over. Between them sits a crudely built table where we spend many of our free hours writing, reading, and gazing at the fold of the mountains to the south.

Our kitchen cabinet is the most sophisticated piece of furniture, with hooks, shelves and lots of nooks and crannies. It is far easier to ration our food into weekly portions and place the bulk condiments into small, airtight tins than to try and rummage through the cache for each particular item. Besides the foodstuffs, this cabinet made of tree stumps, poles and

*The peaks of the Ragged Range*

precious pieces of plywood, contains all our pots, pans and cooking utensils. These hang off pegs above the work counter. Our utensils and cutting knives are set into a simple holder made from a round slab of spruce. The bottom half is six inches thicker than the top, leaving a ledge across the middle. This flat shelf has been chiselled out so that the utensils sit upright in their slots.

The waterjug and fold-up oven have their places on racks beside the cabinet, as does the gold pan which at this moment is doubling as a wash basin. The moose antlers, which John seems to be always dragging home, have been nailed onto a nearby poplar and act as towel racks, coat hooks, and the like.

The door of our sleeping tent opens to the south where the towering pinnacles of the Ragged Range rise behind Snow White. To the rear of the tent is the tool rack and our second equipment tent, which is the library, clothes closet, first aid station and catchall.

One of the last jobs of the day was finding a second fresh water source — one closer to camp. The South Nahanni is not an option, unfortunately. Its silty water is a murky brown colour. Although this probably wouldn't harm us, we haven't the stomachs for mud-coloured tea and gritty bannock. If our plastic water jug didn't have the untimely habit of springing a leak everytime we carry it over the trail we would probably hike the extra distance to secure our drinking water from the arm of the creek.

We discovered what we wanted in the snye that runs alongside our first camp. In one section the Nahanni trickles over a bed of small stones before entering a shallow bay. This grid of pebbles acts as a filter, and the water in the bay is free of silt. Unless the water level changes, we can count on this fresh water supply for the time being.

Having completed our move, we were sitting in our easy chairs admiring the view. I was beginning to feel a little house proud even though the cabin is still just an open floor.

"Everything the way you want it?" John asked.

"Just fine."

I watched the silver lined cumulus tumble across the sky above Snow White. When the sun wasn't behind cloud it shone brightly out of the blue, and the last of the ice sheets, nestled on Snow White's carved ridges, gleamed with light.

"We've got to get up there," I said in a half whisper. "That mountain is simply incredible."

"How about a climb up the cutbank instead?" The suggestion was enough to get me up.

We paddled across the river and beached the canoe on the sandy shore.

Before we had even looked around to figure out the best way to climb up the steep embankment, we noticed a blazed trail. It was a well travelled route, following the shoreline both upstream and down. The blaze marks were not simply scars left by moose or caribou rubbing at the bark, or the result of one tree falling against another — these were man made. The stumps did not have the distinctive profile of a beaver's work — an axe or hatchet had been used.

What was the purpose of a blazed trail in these parts ? How long ago had it been cut? Had Albert Faille, the famous Nahanni prospector, who spent most of his life on the lower portion of the river, travelled this far upstream? Maybe the remains of an old cabin were close by. It was too late to continue exploring if we were going to climb the cutbank, but all these questions begged future exploration.

We left the path at the top of the hill and headed towards the river bank, picking our way through buckbrush and knee high moss that held the previous day's rain like a sponge. At the edge of the cutbank we pushed the boughs of dwarf spruce aside to take in the full view of our site. It was nestled amongst the tapered forms of spruce on the opposite shoreline.

John gasped with pleasure.

Beyond our clearing, nicely set amongst the thicket of forest, was the winding course of Snake Creek. The many contours and elevations of the land surrounding the waterway looked like a relief map set out in front of us. The hill encircling Big Island Lake stood out clearly in contrast to the marshland. We inspected the mountains to the north. The were different in character to those south of us — less bold in their ruggedness and ascent to the sky. Their faces were covered with stands of pine, a rich green velvet in colour. Deep indentations were carved down their slopes, where creek beds poured the melted snows into the valley.

From our vantage point we could scan up and down the river valley and see the lower mountains to the west. They resembled rolling hills compared to the distant Mackenzies.

We could have sat for hours gazing at this lovely and peaceful scene had storm clouds not appeared on the horizon. Too many unprotected belongings could be lost or damaged if the storm reached camp before we did. We scrambled down the path towards home.

We made it into camp before the cloudburst, just before. I scurried around the clearing, gathering armloads of clothing and equipment, and placed them under cover. John lashed the lengths of rope at the bow and stern of the canoe to two large poplars, refastened the tarp cover on the tool rack and checked to see that the kitchen cabinet was properly water-proofed.

The sky was a black stretch of low cloud now, and it was moving in fast. I snatched a book from the equipment tent, grabbed an evening snack on my way to our sleeping tent, and huddled in the warmth of my polar-guard bag. A crack of thunder echoed in the distance just seconds after a streak of light illuminated the ghostly shadows of mountains and hills. Whitecaps danced on the water and foamed on the rocky beach. The slender alders bowed their heads as the winds whipped past them, sometimes carrying away a branch or two. As John stood outside the tent, watching the storm's approach, he was showered with leaves being tossed and tattered into shreds.

The howling wind rendered everything in its path chaotic. John loved to stand and watch.

I was content to observe the commotion from my comfortable dry spot in the tent. It was cozy in there with a candle lit. Nothing short of a tornado would have moved me.

### July 3rd

I awoke suddenly to hear a small animal slide down the nylon fly of the tent. It could have been a mouse, but I suspected it was one of the five baby squirrels who had recently moved into camp. John was quite upset last night to find two of them chewing away on the marrow of his prize moose antler and had angrily chased them away. Now, as I lay in bed, picking mosquitoes out of the air, I could picture the young ones jumping off a nearby tree and sliding gleefully down the slippery fly.

I nudged John and explained what was happening. At first, he politely suggested that I go back to sleep and wake him up once I regained my senses. But when it happened again he immediately reached for the camera case.

"This is going to be tough to get on film, Jo. Should be a classic if we can pull it off though."

Together, we quietly crept out of the tent.

I began to laugh almost immediately and John quickly gave a "be quiet" signal. I could see that we would have to wait a long while for the picture of our dreams — the "squirrels" were really giant poplar seeds, and as I spoke two more fell onto the tent and slid to the ground. Our tent was in a grove of poplar and the seeds were scattering in every direction.

We looked at each other for a moment and then howled.

"Well, nobody can say we don't have any imagination," John said.

The stormy weather had moved on sometime during the night. A cloudless sky greeted us instead of the gloomy overcast of the last four days.

The first day of confinement in the tent had been pleasant. We wrote letters to family and friends, reread the relevant sections of Mackie's book *Building with Logs*, to prepare ourselves for our next stage of building, and caught up on some much needed rest. The next three days found us increasingly restless. A short stint of cutting firewood during a lull in the storm provided some exercise, but the time outside was too brief. The skies lashed out with a driving rain that forced us back inside, this time to the equipment tent, just for a change of scene. We were desparate to get back to work on the cabin.

Immediately after breakfast we took to the woods to fell four or five trees and trim, debark, and cut them. Dragging the logs to the clearing was pure drudgery. John tied a tump line onto the hauling rope and slung it around his forehead for greater pulling power. One branch was left in place so the rope would not slide off the slippery logs. I sunk an axe into the rear end and pulled from behind. If the butt end did not dig into the ground and bring the operation to an abrupt halt, the log would invariably catch on some protruding root. The shallow furrows through the forest, along which we skidded the logs, were getting worn down more each day and this meant new obstacles on every run.

The afternoon was as rewarding as the morning was frustrating, as this was our time for notching the wall logs into place. John worked on the eleven-foot logs on either side of the front door and on the eighteen-foot side wall logs. I concentrated on the nine-foot logs that make up the back walls of the main cabin and the three woodshed walls.

If you had a handful of wooden matches on hand, you could lay out a miniature cabin not unlike ours. The procedure of laying down logs to build up a wall is rather simple, and you soon discover that you can only progress one round up on a wall before the logs on either side must be raised. A good day's work lay behind us if we laid logs the complete distance around. This amounted to setting thirteen logs in place when we were working around the windows and nine when working above and below them.

The logs have to be marked before cutting the notches, and the tool used for this is a scriber. Experts say it originated in Norway where construction with logs dates back to the fourteenth century. Although not absolutely necessary when building — trappers and prospectors certainly managed without them — this tool ensures a tight fitting joint if used with care and accuracy.

Picture an eighteen-foot side wall log, resting on the butt ends of two other logs that lie at right angles to it. In order for it to lie flush against the log beneath it, notches must be cut out of each of its ends. A scriber marks the dimensions of the cross logs onto the inside and outside edges of the log to be placed beneath it.

This compass-like tool is held as near to vertical as possible. The pointed end of the scriber follows the contour of the bottom log — the one on which the eighteen-footer will eventually rest — while the crayon end transfers this information onto the log itself. The scriber is set by spreading the two arms to the same number of inches apart as the widest gap between top and bottom logs. When one side of the eighteen-footer is marked the process is repeated on the other side. When the log is turned over, the crayon lines along its length serve as a cutting guide.

When the log is prepared from end to end it is rolled over and set in place. It should straddle the end logs perfectly and lie flat on the log beneath it.

We collected bagfuls of step-moss for use as chinking material between the logs. This type of filler can be wedged into the seams without resetting the log, but we found it more efficient to roll the log over again, lay handfuls of moss along the entire length of the bottom log and in the round notched areas at the ends, and then carefully reposition the top log. The moss has insects in it, but they move out once it dries.

When working, we wear lightweight fishnet bug jackets soaked in citronella. They are extremely efficient in keeping the bugs at bay. When using sharp tools protection of this sort is a must. An untimely assault by a blackfly when you have an axe, adze, or chainsaw in hand, could end in disaster!

There is something uniquely comforting in seeing the walls of our home rise daily, knowing that the construction techniques are our own.

We have our share of leisure hours, but only after the site is thoroughly cleaned up and an inventory check of our tools completed. This includes maintenance as well. Our building tools require constant attention, because if they break down we're out of luck. While John is no mechanic he is learning fast and has already performed admirable surgery on one of the chainsaws. The choke pull snapped and he fashioned a new one from a piece of wire. He covered it with tape to match the original in size and to prevent dust from entering the air filter chamber. This innovative design seems more reliable than the plastic original.

Less mechanical in nature but equally frustrating are repairs to axe, adze, hammer and sledge. Already, several new handles have been whittled for these tools.

One evening John carved a new hammer handle from a piece of poplar — a long tedious exercise. To test the finished product he hammered a nail into a nearby block of wood. The handle cracked in two on the first blow.

He was so angry that I made myself scarce for a while. The next time I saw him he was returning from the woods with a branch of a seasoned birch in hand. This harder wood survived the preliminary test and is still intact.

# Visitors — Airborne and Afloat

*July 7th*

It is just a personal idiosyncrasy, but I always hoped we would be hard at work when travellers arrived, not loafing in our easy chairs as we were doing this afternoon when two red canoes appeared. A voice, deep, and friendly, boomed into the clearing.

"Looks like you two have got yourselves a little slice of heaven there!"

This perfect description of our surroundings, and our place in them, came from a bearded fellow who introduced himself as Bruce. He looked more like a trapper than the doctor from Whitehorse he said he was. The other members of the foursome were Roger (a doctor as well), Bruce's wife Jean, and Sharon (both nurses).

I hadn't seen a member of my own sex in five weeks so it wasn't any time before I was immersed in conversation with the women, while John talked with Roger and Bruce.

When we learned Roger had attended Queen's University, as we had, we began to pump him with all the questions we had been embarrassed to ask the bush pilots. What weather conditions could we expect during the winter months? How much snow? How long could we safely stay outdoors in sixty below temperatures? A transplanted southerner could better understand our ignorance.

We were as interested to hear details of the group's travels and the scenery on the upper portion of the South Nahanni as they were inquisitive about our reasons for building a cabin on its shores. We welcomed the news reports they offered too, for we were already noticing the absence of newspapers and the six o'clock television report.

Bruce and Jean were newlyweds. This was their first whitewater adventure and they had embarked on it only hours after being married. When they heard our story there was kidding all around.

When John and I were leaving on our trip we were targets for such comments as: "One winter in isolation is worth twenty-five years of marriage," or "You'll either return from the bush bound together for life or

55

you'll never want to see each other again." Our visitors had heard their own versions of these jokes even more recently.

The visit was a short one. John and I waved from the riverbank as the two canoes disappeared around the bend. It was a bit like a dream. One minute the clearing was absolutely still and other human beings seemed miles away, then the excitement of a meeting and the pleasure of sharing stories over tea, and then — absolute quiet again.

Roger had given us a tip though. "You'll kick yourself if you rush putting on the roof. Go that extra round of logs or you'll be bumping into rafters and the top of the door frame all winter long." This sensible advice we remembered.

"Well Jo, we can sit in our chairs and there's bound to be someone come along sometime — or we can get at those walls."

"The walls," I answered. "So we can paddle upriver a way before dinner."

When a round of logs was laid and the building tools cleaned up, we took off for some water travel of our own. Our trusty aluminum canoe had proved its durability during the Snake Creek runs, now we'd see how well it performed in faster water.

We realized the minute we were afloat that if we wasted a second sitting idle, the surge of current would carry the canoe downstream. The South Nahanni is like a treadmill in constant motion, and paddling against the flow means tearing at the water with each stroke. There wasn't even time to breath in between.

"Dig, dig, dig," John shouted. "Power it out Jo. Power. Power!"

The canoe crawled forward. We were out in midchannel where the water was well over our heads, but once past the edge of the clearing we could creep closer to shore again. I kept a lookout from the bow for exposed rocks or shallow sections when we moved to cut into slacker water. We used the shoreline as a reference point to judge our progress.

"A rock to our right, John!" I bellowed. "We have to go left around it."

"Keep the bow tucked into shore," John yelled back," or the current will grab it and send us back home. I'm going to try the pole. You paddle until I get a grip on this thing."

Before we left camp, John had cut a seventeen-foot spruce and tapered the end of it so he could use it as a pole. As he sank the tip of it into the water, a surge of current caught it and the lower end flailed about for a few precious seconds. Finally it sank between a crevice in the rocks below the surface.

I was paddling furiously to maintain our position, all the while keeping an eye on the exposed rock shelf in front of us. We were losing ground.

John heaved on the pole with all his strength. The bow of the canoe rode high over the waves and we crept forward.

We repeated this routine for over an hour before we sighted a sandy beach and ran the canoe up onto it. We had covered less than half a mile.

It wasn't the distance that mattered though; it was getting a feel for the river and knowing that we could travel upstream whenever we chose to that was important. The South Nahanni could be as much of a highway for us as the game trails were, once we developed some method of travelling against the vigorous flow.

*July 11th*

A minor calamity occurred yesterday, necessitating some alterations in cabin design before we took to the woods today for more logs.

A wall of black threatening sky had moved in early in the day, along with strong winds from the east. The onset of the storm had irritated us, because it meant we'd be confined to the tent again. The hours spent staring at the green nylon walls and listening to the drum of the rain had become intolerable. One more minute in the tent, other than for sleep, would have driven us mad, so we set up a canopy using the last protective covering we had available — the panes of plexiglass.

We set the eight sheets on two parallel poles supported on tripods. This shelter allowed us to work at our table while the icy rain thundered down from the heavens. The deluge continued for the rest of the day, but we were quite content, sharpening tools, sewing patches on our work clothes, reading and writing.

When the worst of the storm had subsided, by dinner time, the winds picked up considerably. Neither of us gave it a thought until a blast of wind caught the edge of one four-foot-square sheet and sent it hurtling to the ground by the woodpile. A piece of the windowpane splintered leaving three-quarters of the original intact.

Before any logs could be placed today we had to modify the size of the window frame already set into the wall. The bottom and top pieces were cut down to the proper size, and the upright supports were repositioned.

It was only a minor mishap, but we were again reminded of the cost of doing foolish things. If the entire wall had already been built around the window frame we would have had to dismantle several rounds of logs to correct the error.

Representatives of Lands and Forests flew in late in the afternoon. We were returning from the bush carrying short logs for use around the windows when the helicopter landed on the rocky bar. The visit was

*John working on window sills*

strictly business. The men were there to check our campsite for cleanliness and to ensure that we were obeying departmental regulations about fire prevention and conservation of the land.

We were told that a charge of fifty cents a cord is usually imposed, but as husband and wife we qualified for fifty free cords of wood. However, there was going to be a charge for our building logs. When John asked the charge for a seven-inch-diameter log, eighteen feet long, the rather stern gentleman answered, "Hmmm, I guess about three and a half cents." A quick mental calculation and we arrived at a figure in the neighbourhood of six dollars for the whole building.

"That's six dollars I don't think we have." John whispered to me.

The authorities were not concerned about collecting that day which was all for the best. I had a grand total of three dollars and fifty-four cents to my name and John was penniless.

When the helicopter lifted our newest guests away we felt somewhat relieved. The air of government officialdom surrounding this particular visit seemed totally alien to our environment. The men were friendly, but once the helicopter was out of sight we breathed easily again and broke into laughter.

"We must be really bushed." John chuckled.

*July 13th*

The day was cold and windy, and it looked as though we might get more rain. We emerged from the tent clad from head to toe in the warmest clothes we could find — not easy, as most of our cold weather gear was packed away. Who would have thought that down jackets would be needed at this time of year. John summed up the day in a word. "Miserable!" he growled as he scrambled off to the woods to find dry tinder for the morning fire.

Our faces and hands were flushed with colour from the hot flames we huddled close to, but a bone chilling wind crept up our backs. I filled our largest pail with water and balanced it on the fire irons to heat up. We'd be making several trips back to camp for hot tea. John stacked some kindling next to the pit so we could add pieces when the coals began to die. This done, we collected our tools and headed to the forest for logs.

We carried shorter lengths into camp now, balancing them on our shoulders and dropping them where they would be used — around the door and window frames. We worked alone when cutting and cleaning these logs, but once at the cabin it was a team effort to cut and place them at a level above our waists. Each new round of logs now changed the cabin's appearance; it was taking on a definite shape.

We aren't referring to building texts much any more and this allows more time for other activities. I use the lunch hours to tend my garden — a first green thumb attempt — or catch up on baking breads or desserts. Enormous quantities of these are devoured at each meal, along with our regular fare.

I discovered very quickly that baking in my wilderness kitchen is a very different procedure than I was accustomed to in the city. My days of setting the stove at a required temperature, whipping up a batter of sorts, setting a timer and then going about activities while my latest concoction baked are long gone. Cooking on an open fire, using a fold-up oven, is a specialized art.

The problem is to maintain the right heat for the proper length of time, and my first attempts were miserable failures. I find that raising and lowering the oven over a set fire is the best method. I have to man my post next to the fire for the duration of the cooking time, but the finished product is appetizing and I have lots of time to further refine the process.

Bread or dessert recipes requiring yeast as a leavening agent are the most challenging to make, because to maintain the right temperature for the dough to rise properly, I have to adapt my techniques to changes in the weather. On hot sunny days the inside of the tent is the perfect temperature to activate the yeast; on cold or rainy days I have to work a little harder. I heat the coleman oven over the coals, let it cool down to the "warm" reading on the oven's dial and then set it on a pole rack in the equipment tent, away from any drafts. I set the dough inside and after an hour punch it down while the oven reheats for the second hour of rising. Following this the oven goes directly from the equipment tent to the hot bed of coals for the required cooking time.

Besides learning these new baking techniques I have had to rethink quantity. Our caloric intakes are close to five thousand and three thousand calories daily. Our freeze-dried meats have very little fat so any deficiency is made up in rich biscuits, with margarine and sweet desserts. Back home I wouldn't dream of touching these, and now I go back for third helpings at a meal! John is simply amazing — whatever number of muffins, breads, cakes and pastries I serve, he eats.

In planning the master menu for the trip I allowed for a substantial increase in our appetites,especially during this building period, so I'm less worried about having enough staples than running out of new ideas and the time to bake such large quantities. Rest days, it seems, are going to have to be turned into colossal baking sprees, unless I resign myself to making these extras every day.

When work for the day ended, I took to the kitchen. This afternoon, while I tended the fire, I made up a list of supplies we needed in camp. One trip a week to the "Dominion Store" (a further example of our fetish for naming things) is enough to stock the canisters with staples and the shelves with canned goods. Limiting the shopping trip to once a week makes it much easier to maintain a close watch on rations. Although the menu was planned to allow for generous meals, the amounts of each staple item still have to be noted. I'm not keeping as scrupulous a check on our dwindling larder as will probably become necessary a few months from now.

The weekly grocery excursion is usually a joint effort, but John was deeply involved in his latest book today, so I went alone. The oatmeal squares were cooling on the counter as I gathered up the canoe packs and strolled down the path.

I returned to a debacle. While John read on, in relaxed oblivion, the local red squirrels had had a feast. They were like bandits on the run when I chased them off with the broom, but I no sooner turned my back than they were back for more. The forest's telegraph system works well. Just let one squirrel try a nibble of oatmeal square and his entire family shows up.

The raucous chatter and confusion in the tree tops intensified. Bushy tails wagged while five furry faces peering down at us tried to figure out where the pan of sweets had disappeared to. I had hidden them in the oven and set the door latch firmly, defying one of the varmints to try and get one now.

For several minutes not a squirrel moved. The silence was so absolute we wondered what had prompted the ceasefire. Then we saw the reason — a hungry hunter on the prowl.

The dark form in the undergrowth moved gracefully from one bush to the next. The inquisitive, beady eyes searched long and hard before the short legs pounced forward. The beautiful heart-shaped face and silky coat of fur on our newest visitor confirmed our suspicion that it was a marten. His steps were quick but measured, his back slightly arched, as he slunk to the woodpile. He paid no heed to the frantic exodus of squirrels, nor to John and me. We stayed quite still. Our guest was after the oatmeal squares.

We watched in disbelief while the marten crept closer to the small oven like a household pussycat, straddled it, sniffed at the airholes, and pawed at the door latch for several minutes. When he retreated to the woodpile again it was only to reevaluate the situation. He soon returned for another snoop and a try at scratching his way through the lightweight sheet of aluminum. Finally, a hissing growl erupted from his throat, but the show of disgust was not directed at John and me. Our visitor was clearly peeved;

not only was the latch impossible to figure out but the stove itself sat firmly
on the ground despite all attempts to knock it over.

*July 17th*
It's not often one's instructor comes more than three thousand miles to
pay a visit and check your work firsthand, and had John and I been anywhere else but on the South Nahanni River, I doubt that Chris could have
justified the expense. It was possible because he and Gary, the director of
a camp John attended as a young teenager, were leading a group of canoeists on a whitewater adventure down the river. When we announced
that we were going north, Chris incorporated a cabin building bee into
the group's itinerary. Chris' presence at a time when John and I are probably the most difficult, if not the most expensive, couple to visit, is truly
an event. His impending arrival was a motivating force behind our construction efforts, spurring us on to greater achievements.

You would have to have seen Chris' expression on landing at the beach
to fully appreciate how he must have felt. He climbed out of his canoe,
stretched out his arms in welcome, and produced the warmest smile ever.
We were so choked up when we heard the "Wow" roll off his tongue that
we were speechless — and slightly embarrassed in front of the eleven other
members of the party. They were standing in water, next to their canoes,
trying, I sensed, not to feel too uncomfortable during this private moment. While we moved forward to greet them, Chris inspected the half-
finished cabin more closely.

We knew alsolutely nothing about building a cabin — felling a tree
even — when Chris took us in hand, so I can understand his pleasure on
seeing that our home was not a haphazard arrangement of crooked trees
and gaping holes. His appreciative exclamation was the finest flattery we
could have asked for.

Our visitors were eager to get going on cabin work, so after lunch we led
the way into the forest.

The hours slipped by unnoticed once the building bee was underway.
The forest thundered with the sounds of axes, saws and falling trees. The
clearing was a hubbub of activity too. John, along with several of the men,
dropped one spruce after another. These were then hauled into camp
where a group waited to strip them clean.

After dinner, the music of Chris' guitar and Gary's harmonica, the
sound of our voices raised in song and the roar of a crackling bonfire filled
the clearing. John and I relished every moment of it, even when at times
we felt ourselves sensitive to the noise and the stimulation of so many

*A red squirrel into the oatmeal squares*

people. We fell into the tent that night too exhausted from talking and working to care about a thing.

*July 18th*

From the time we set to work after breakfast until the day's work was declared finished, the cabin area was buzzing. Anyone not working at the moment had their camera equipment out, filming "the story of the log" — the steps that are necessary to convert a noble spruce tree to a cleaned and notched log in the cabin wall. John and I still recall our excitement over learning how to build, so the sharing of information was an exhilarating opportunity for us.

By evening, thirty stripped logs — enough to complete the cabin walls — lay strewn amongst tents, food packs, upturned canoes, and fourteen sunburnt bodies. What remains for John and me in the weeks ahead is to notch the logs, raise the walls of our home, and then put a roof on.

The faces of our guests were jubilant. They had thrown themselves wholeheartedly into a chore that was, for many, a totally new experience. It was with a great sense of pride that they carved out their names in some of the logs, as reminders of their contribution. In a day and a half, they had completed a job that would have meant an extra week's work for John and myself.

During the day's efforts I kept a watchful eye on Chris' dad, Chuck, a tall man with rugged good looks, a crop of snowy white hair, and the energy of youth flowing through his viens. His character emerged strongly during the two days, expressed mainly through his fine skills as a builder. He was in his element. The strong bond of friendship between him and Chris intrigued me, as did his age. I wasn't so bold as to ask him how old he was, but the question was close to surfacing a couple of times, especially during his antics of removing logs from the forest. He strode regally out of the woods with a nine foot log balancing on his right shoulder, as the rest of us milled around the clearing near the end of the day. When asked if that was his way of finishing up a day's work, he said he was returning for another — his left shoulder was riding too high. He is a man far younger than his years. I can only wish for his spirit and vitality in my own lifetime.

Another of our visitors who has retained his vivacity and love for people, is Gary. His skills, mastered from years of directing YMCA camps, were called upon tonight. He was asked to lead the group in song and lead us he did! His memorable rendition of "The Cremation of Sam McGee," to the tune of "Val-der-Ree," was the highlight of the evening for me.

Following this was a comic presentation of a modest cake to celebrate Gary's fiftieth birthday. We had baked an oversized shortbread cookie and crowned it with one of our lantern candles.

*July 19th*

The morning was glorious — sunny and cloudless. The temperature was already soaring when we all collected for breakfast, some muttering that Chuck's morning yodel (a Paul Bunyan call) had disturbed a perfectly blissful sleep. Our friends would be on their way shortly after the morning meal.

Organizing the food and equipment to load into the canoes took the better part of two hours, but somehow the right packs ended up in the right canoes. Soon the six Grummans were aligned on shore, loaded to the brim and ready to go.

"We need a group picture," someone called out over the din of conversation, and in a moment day packs were opened and cameras uncovered. Any reason to postpone the inevitable departure suited me just fine. I joined the others in front of the cabin.

The front of the clearing resembled a Warner Brothers' set with the assortment of cameras and tripods crowded together there. While twelve of us held casual poses and wide grins, two runners manned the timers and then ran into the picture. This last formality attended to, the group started on its way.

A chorus of Happy Birthdays, Merry Christmases and Happy New Years started up while John and I remained on the rocky beach with lumps in our throats, unable to respond for a minute or two. We waved goodbye as the canoes drifted out of sight, then turned towards an empty camp.

For the remainder of the day we set logs into place, but our minds were only half on our work. We laughed as we recalled certain events — the previous day's clamour to see who used the bathtub first, the singsongs, the special foods we enjoyed and wouldn't see again for quite a while, the teamwork, the cribbage tournaments, the discovery that John and I had somehow lost a day over the course of our first six weeks in the valley. These memories would linger on.

*July 22nd*

Temperatures are rising daily. At 4 a.m. the thermometer outside registered twenty-seven degrees celsius. It was unbearable in the tent, so we rose early. We had five more logs to notch, and then we could begin the rafters and gable ends.

Late in the morning I was turning a corner of the cabin, trying to un-cover a lost set of scribers in the pile of sawdust, when a voice bid me "Hello." I was startled but managed a "Good Morning," realizing, after I said it, that it seemed more like late afternoon to me. Our newest visitor was on foot. He explained that he and the seven others in his party had landed at Big Island Lake. Our orange markers through the maze of channels in Snake Creek had led them to the site.

As the day's weather was deteriorating rapidly, we invited this group to camp overnight in the clearing. They arranged their camp next to ours while John and I worked. During coffee breaks we visited with them.

At 3 p.m. six canoes pulled up in front of the cabin, a family expedition from Peterborough, Ontario. They stayed only long enough to visit brief-ly and then continued downriver. They were trying to put in as many miles as possible.

Just as the Peterborough entourage left, six more canoes appeared, this time twelve campers from Ontario's Camp Wanapetai. Malcolm, the leader of the group, corralled everyone into line behind John and off they went on a tour of the cabin and cache. Questions flowed as one thing or another caught their eye. These teenagers were all keenly interested in our plans, the construction techniques we used in the cabin, and how we'd planned our trip. I was impressed with their knowledge about home-steading and the wilderness life.

When the clearing was restored to normalcy again, our Alberta visitors jokingly asked if thirty-two visitors in one day was a common occurrence.

At the end of the day, we picked up a lesson in building a "sweat lodge" — an Indian style sauna. A circular area of ground about six to eight feet in diameter is levelled off and eight holes are made around its circumfer-ence, using a stout peg. A pit is dug within the area to a depth of one and a half feet. Eight ten-foot-long alder or willow branches are selected and trimmed, leaving the foliage on the end. The butts of the branches are whittled to a point, and driven into the holes in the ground. Alders from opposite sides are bent inwards and secured together by weaving the foli-aged ends. This makes a domed structure that can be strengthened by weaving other alders throughout.

An opening is left at either end of the superstructure, one an entrance-way, the other an opening through which heated rocks can be passed into the pit.

A non-breathable plastic or thick canvas tarpaulin covers the dome. It is arranged so the front and back entrances are flapped — for easy entrance and exit, but also to make it airtight when in use.

The rocks can be heating up while the lodge is under construction. A crib is made out of large diameter logs, leaving enough area in the centre to allow for plenty of kindling and driftwood to be jammed in. A flat roof of logs covers the crib, and stones are set on it to be heated. The fire should be tended to regularly to keep as much heat under the rocks as possible. Dry rocks should be used, because they are less likely to expand at high temperatures. Wet or cracked stones may splinter and throw off fragments.

When the rocks are red hot they are shovelled into the pit, where water is dribbled over them. We found the steam to be almost suffocating, but a splash of cold water on the face or even a moment spent with our faces down in the pail allowed us to remain in the lodge for a longer time. When we'd had our fill we leapt into the river.

Our visitors had given us new knowledge and a delightful addition to our camp. On a glacier-fed river, such as the South Nahanni, whose waters are cold enough to deter even the heartiest of souls, a sauna is a must. I had not set a toe in the river for fear of freezing to death, but five minutes in the sweat lodge and I was more than eager to take the plunge.

John and I were told that experienced "sweaters" can last for several rounds. I could only take two. After a second dip in the river, I downed four cups of delicious hot tea, hit the sleeping bag and didn't hear a sound until morning. It was the dreamiest sleep ever.

*July 24th*
John rose at 6 a.m. to relieve himself and decided to stay up. He fixed himself a batch of pancakes and then went down to a spot along the river we had affectionately named "Ted's Fishing Hole." This pool of deep, still water was named in honour of one of our sweat lodge builders — the fisherman of the group.

After more than an hour with no luck he was ready to call it quits, when he noticed signs of movement in the water. A monstrous fish was just about to nab the lure as he prepared to reel in the last few feet so he let it dangle for a second more. The big Dolly Varden took it.

When he returned to camp he was beaming from ear to ear and posed with the Dolly Varden — all ten pounds of it. It measured thirty-one inches from tip to tail.

Breakfast that morning was long and hearty, a good thing, because after we exchanged addresses with our latest visitors and bid them a safe

*John's prize ten-pound Dolly Varden*

journey, we went straight to work. Not a moment was wasted all day. Our home was too near completion for us to think of anything else but getting the roof on and moving in.

By late evening the top wall logs, two twenty-five-footers, which the sweat lodge builders had kindly helped us raise, were notched. Several birch logs, which we had split into half rounds, now framed the windows. A medium size spruce, cut into quarter rounds, was nailed along the base of the floor where it met the walls. These simple additions, nailed over seams generously stuffed with moss first, will minimize the draft.

After dinner, we placed the rafters at either end of the cabin. Just as we had laid the floor boards on a support shelf, we now set eight poles on shelves cut in the end of each plate log. Our year's supply of food and equipment will eventually be moved into these attics for the winter months.

*July 31st*

Canoeists continue to drop into the site for tea and conservation, but their numbers are dwindling.

The days of sunshine and warm weather that follow one after the other see the level of the South Nahanni dropping considerably. In another couple of weeks the upper reaches of the river won't have enough water flowing between their banks to float a rubber duck, let alone a loaded canoe. From the reports we have gathered, August will be a slow month, and by September the valley will again be our own silent world.

Our work schedule has picked up considerably in the past week. The gable ends of each side wall of the cabin were raised to support two purlins and the ridgepole, the poles forming the superstructure of the roof. Finally, all that remained was to nail down the roof poles — all two hundred and fifty of them.

Finding this number of twelve-foot-long spruce was more monotonous than difficult, but we were at the stage of building where we performed like two pre-programmed robots. Up in the early hours of dawn, eat, take axe in hand, head to the forest to cut down trees and haul them to the site, then back for more. Many days my arms and legs ached so, I feared I was growing weaker, rather than stronger. But unlike the earlier days, when I would take a longer lunch break to recuperate, I wouldn't allow myself that luxury now. Our time to reap the benefits of our labor is so close. We'll have time to scale the mountain slopes and explore new places as soon as the cabin is complete.

Once half the number of poles were nailed to the roof structure, we went ahead with the second, third and fourth roof layers. Two hundred green garbage bags of moss were needed for this. Generous amounts of stepmoss were wedged into the cracks between the logs. Strips of tarpaper were then nailed down as a waterproof barrier and covered with a layer of moss six to eight inches thick. Last came the sods — more than a hundred foot-and-a-half square sheets of earth and roots, laid down like roof shingles so the rain would drain off properly.

When we tired of doing the roof we busied ourselves with setting up the stove, cutting birch poles for furniture, or hewing boards for the front door.

It was a great moment when our Lakewood Stepstove, an airtight model, took its place of honour in the centre of the cabin. Our central heater-oven-stove sits in a square framework of logs filled with stones and silt. We installed the firebricks and connected the lengths of stove piping through a circular opening in the roof.

A bridge of spruce poles holds our insulated stovepipe and chimney in place. We added extra reinforcement around the stack and as many screw nails as we had available so the special brackets of aluminum flashing were held securely in place, inside and out. If there was any doubt about how strong a section of the roof was, we'd nail a second barrier down. "This one's for the wolverines!" was the most overworked phrase of the day. By the time we screwed the chimney cap in place, we defied one of the culprits to get in.

The same thinking applied to the front door — another animal access route into the cabin. We cut and fitted jambs on the four sides of the opening, smoothing the inside edges with the adze so the door would fit snugly into the groove. The door itself was four half rounds hewed down to two-and-a-half-inch-thick planks that were held together by half round crosspieces bolted on the inside. To prevent drafts from seeping through the seams, we stuffed moss in between and nailed half rounds over top. The birch pieces, against the clean white spruce planks, form a lattice that reminds me of Tudor-style homes. A touch of class!

*August 4th*

Some of our letters took months to reach home, but as long as there were canoeists on the river we had a means of communicating with our family and friends. Last night we stayed up long after our latest visitors had retired to their tents, getting the last of the mail together. When our four male guests continued on their journey the next morning, they carried with them the most valuable parcels we could send out — the news that our cabin was built. With one of these letters was film, to show everyone what it was we were moving into.

*The Lakewood Stepstove takes its place of honour*

Our first home is no candidate for *Better Homes and Gardens*, but to John and me it is the ultimate in comfort. The roof, with all its layers of moss, tarpaper and sods, is tight as a drum. The stove works well and the door swings straight on its hinges. It is a dream come true.

The cabin's interior is still unfinished, but the basics of furniture are well underway. We have divided the cabin into four rooms: the kitchen area, the dining-living room area, our bedroom, and a dressing-washing area — each occupies a corner of the cabin.

When building the framework for our cabinets we used birch, a strong wood that resists warping and wear. The L-shaped kitchen cabinet, built into the northeast wall, is a countertop with shelves above and below. The plywood sheets we brought in with us were cut to fit the framework exactly and nailed on top. In the centre of one of these sheets we cut a twelve-inch-square hole, so our plastic washbasin would fit in and act as a sink. A length of heavy plastic tubing runs from a hole in the bottom of the basin to a tunnel underground.

The kitchen table is a simple structure of birch poles with a sheet of stained and varnished plywood nailed to the top. Around this are two log chairs — or "ten ton chairs" as we call them — the largest diameter spruce logs we could find, with a longitudinal portion cut out of them so we have a ledge to sit on and back supports.

Against the south wall we have set hewn planks atop foot-long logs, to serve as a bookshelf. Our books, the camera, binoculars, and the diary are kept safe and sound here.

Our bed occupies the southwest corner of the cabin. It is a five-by-six-foot monstrosity raised about two feet off the floor, so we can use the space underneath for storage. The bed posts are large peeled spruce logs, set upright at each of the four corners. Mortised and tenoned to these at the head and foot of the bed are six-foot-long poles to which a number of half rounds, running widthwise, are notched and nailed. We have a slab of foam that lies across these crosspieces and our collection of sleeping bags and eiderdowns.

Next to the bed, running the length of the west wall, and in front of our largest picture window, is an eight-foot counter that doubles as writing desk and washstand. We have set our gold pan and a mirror on the end closest to our bureau and closet, so that the northwest corner of the cabin can be made into a semi-private washing or dressing area if necessary.

Our most treasured pieces of furniture are the closet and bureau, because we have lived out of canvas bags so long that we are sick to death of rummaging through them to find the smallest item.

*Inside the cabin*

The bureau is a classic piece suited for cabin living and cabin living alone! We built four open cubicles out of birch poles and half rounds and slid durable cardboard boxes into them. The design of this cabinet isn't what catches your eye when you walk into the cabin, it is the four four-by-six-inch Chiquita Banana labels on the front of the boxes. They have already made visitors wince and take a second look.

# Wilderness Trails

The early days of August were devoted to completing last minute details of cabin and furniture; this done, we thought of only one thing — the time had come to don our backpacks and head into the higher country. Our afternoon hikes through the hushed forests and up the timbered slopes behind the cabin had merely served to whet our appetites. We would climb a ridge to eat lunch at some place from which we could eye the clearing. The cabin looked so snug, nestled amongst the tall spruce. The sight of it reaffirmed what we had always believed — this was the life for us.

Sometimes we sat for long periods in the lee of a rock face, or crouched against a windfall on the ridge of a hill and studied the far off slopes through our binoculars, for signs of game. The reflective times spent curled up in a bed of moss while the sun's rays slipped through a ceiling of spruce boughs and played their light on the lush growth at our feet were occasions of close communion with our wild surroundings.

We pored over topographic maps in the evenings, studying elevations, contours and map symbols — all the interpretative details important for hiking. We planned menus, repaired equipment, and talked of how far and how long our hikes would be.

Then, in the midst of our preparation, we received news of a tragedy that sobered us to the dangers of choosing untrodden paths. A second group of Camp Wanapetai trippers arrived, bringing with them the sad report that Malcolm, the leader of the first party that had visited our site, was missing and presumed dead. An intensive search had been carried out when it was discovered that Malcolm had not returned to his group's camp near Virginia Falls, the South Nahanni's 294-foot cataract. He had wandered off alone, to investigate the canyons beyond that point.

We took a few days off from our packing and cut two cords of winter wood, a needed addition to camp, though that wasn't our reason for putting our energies into the task. We were badly in want of a diversion — something to dwell on other than Malcolm's fate and the message it emphasized: the hazards of heading out alone into a country we were not yet totally familiar with.

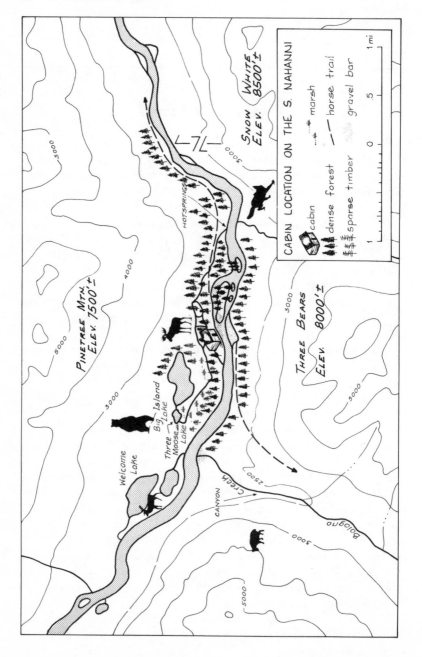

It took several days of contemplation before the urge to travel returned, but we used the time to our advantage, rechecking the outfit and cleaning up the site. Our spirits restored, we put the final touchs to our plans.

The cabin would be secure during our lengthy absences, now that shutters were made for each window and a scheme devised to lock the cabin.

We had cut a foot-and-a-half-square trapdoor in one of the woodshed walls so we could bolt the front door shut from the inside and crawl out through the opening which acted as our rear exit. From inside, the trapdoor closed with a latch and it had no handle or lock on the outside. A birch pole was set in a groove on the inside wall of the woodshed and rested on a shelf on the back of the trapdoor. We could manipulate the pole by a rope attachment that went through a hole in the wall next to the small door. Only a knotted end showed on the outside of the wall when the pole was firmly set. Unravelling the knot and pulling hard on the rope would free the pole and drop the hinged doorway. Unless the local wildlife could read our note explaining how the system worked, the cabin and its contents were safe. As for closing up after we had crawled through the opening ourselves, we merely let go of the rope quickly and the pole fell into place.

*August 17th*

We were up at 6 a.m. raring to go, despite the inclement weather — cloudy, windy and twenty degrees Celsius. As was usual on days we intended to work long hours, we stacked the pancakes in heaps on our plates and doused them with butter and maple syrup. We would need extra fuel; the first day of climbing was always the toughest.

Our loads weighed forty and sixty pounds, approximately one-third our respective body weights, and contained tent, sleeping bags, clothes, five day's food, camera equipment, and an assortment of cutlery, pots, bug repellent and other such necessary items. Once the canoe and paddles were stashed in the bush on the opposite bank, we hoisted the packs on our shoulders and fell into step.

The morning's trek was a slow, steady climb up the Three Bears, westward towards Bologna Creek Canyon. From an earlier outing we knew that the blaze marks that had so intrigued us would lead us into the pass for at least three miles. Now, our plan was to follow the worn path through the dense timber and up the slope for a greater distance. How far we would go depended on what conditions lay ahead.

By noon we had topped a steep ridge and decided to break for lunch. The path had led us up a series of treed terraces, some very steep and tiring to climb. Now these fell 1500 feet below us like long steps, appearing

*A hike into Bologna Creek Canyon*

infinitely easier to ascend than they actually were. Beside us was a stream bed, gushing an icy cold runoff where we could refill our water bottles, and a nice strip of moss and clover to fall into while the soup simmered on the Optimus, our lightweight gas stove.

After lunch, instead of climbing higher we cut across the ridge into Bologna Creek Pass. The blazed path we followed was like a roller coaster — down through spruce forest and up the side of rocky cliffs. Many miles of it lay behind us when we began to look for a suitable campsite.

Just when the packs began feeling overly burdensome, and our shoulders and hips were crying out for relief, we approached a wide creek bed, one of the many that gouged a path out of the side of the mountain. Twin cascades of water tumbled off a smooth ledge above us, one curtain of foam and sparkling water jetting straight down twenty feet, the other, having worn a groove out of the softer rock, weaving through the cracks and around the juts. At our feet was a pool of deep blue water, about as cold as a liquid can get. Camp, we agreed, could be set up on a flat rock shelf next to the falls, with the tent opening facing the mountains to the west.

We levelled an area for our tent by laying armloads of stepmoss in the dips and hollows. Our ensolite pads (inch thick closed cell foam) and sleeping bags were set atop this cushion and a fire built in front of the tent opening. The semicircle of rock slabs was piled high and close together so the heat from the fire would reflect off the rocks and direct its warmth our way. You couldn't ask for a finer arrangement.

The pile of dry wood snapped to life in seconds, sending up a spray of sparks and long arms of orange light. Camp was in the shadow of the rock wall behind us, where the water gurgled softly over the ledges. The sparkle of our fire lit up the shiny wet surfaces of rock and the line of dark forest on either side of us. We lazed over a long dinner of soup, freeze-dried meat and vegetables, bannock and pudding, watching while darkness descended on the basin of forest and the evening shadows played light tricks on the higher outcroppings.

*August 18th*
Before hitting the trail, we piled what was not needed for the day's excursion into the tent and set kindling aside under a small tarp. Camp set-up would remain as a base so we could fan out in different directions over the next few days without having to wear our packs.

We began the day intending to continue along the trail, but on the far side of the creek we began following false blazes. These were most likely caused by animals — moose or caribou — rubbing their antlers against the bark. We laboured through patches of wet moss and became entangled in brush, trying to find our way. About four hundred feet higher, we sat down on a ledge of granite to study the situation. We knew we were not on a trail, but we decided against turning back and starting over. It was a sunny day, so we'd try for the summit. We could scale the bare rock that loomed above us or continue through the brush. Even though climbing through clumps of alder slowed our progress, it was safer travelling. One bypass around a particularly thick patch of the stuff led us up a treacherous rockslide where we took to all fours. Once was enough of that! I was too terrified to even look behind or remain on a rock outcropping for very long. My heart was racing when we made it past the slide, and unless it was absolutely necessary, I wasn't keen on trying my luck again.

By noon we estimated our elevation at six thousand feet. We were on a ledge in the lee of a rock wall formed by gigantic boulders, overlooking a slide of shale slabs we had detoured around. To our left was a deep gorge. Out of the grassy depths of this gully rose an austere tower of rock, and from one of its protective enclosures we could hear the mutterings of a marmot. Soaring above the needle sharp points was an eagle, its screeches echoing in the barren surroundings.

After a hot lunch we climbed higher still by traversing a section of loose shale, then along a worn path on the very crown of the ridge. We eased our way along this, watching every step, because the mountain dropped off sharply on either side. One careless move and we would go sliding down a scree of loose gravel and stone onto a tiny ledge a good hundred feet below.

Negotiating this rise was worth the risk in the end. It led to a mountain meadow, a sea of wild flowers and grasses, gently swaying in the breeze. From the minute we set foot on this lovely flatland, I was overcome by the feeling that I was on top of the world. It was breathtaking — the spaciousness, the alpine air so clean and vibrant, the grass covered slopes we ran up so rounded and gentle in comparison to the raw edges of the far off peaks.

We laughed and sang strains from "The Sound of Music," posed for pictures and ran through the meadow whooping and hollering. On this afternoon, the hills were alive — with the sounds of two happy people sharing a most precious experience!

Not until the last possible moment did we make our way home, following the gentler slope of the southern ridge.

*Sound of Music*

*August 21st*

We woke to find a rim of ice on the water bucket and more snow on the crests of the mountains. We decided to return to the cabin for warmer clothing. A day in camp to clean the outfit and we would continue our travels, this time up the river to the Little Nahanni River and points beyond.

We finished up the last of the flour and oatmeal by adding baking powder, salt, a couple of spoonfuls of powdered E-Z egg, and milk, then frying the concoction in butter. A liberal dab of jam spread on this rich biscuit and you have yourself a fine morning meal.

We feasted on berries all the way home, forgetting our vow that we would fill all the empty containers we had with fruit, so I could bake pies.

The rose hips were in bloom, but they were not yet ready to be picked. Later in August, when the nights became frosty, would be a better time. Then they would be ripe enough to use in preserves. I had a recipe for marmalade I was anxious to try out.

One of the exciting finds on our way into the pass had been an old blanket covered with moss and dirt, lying to one side of the trail. We left it there intending to poke around the undergrowth on our return. We nicked several trees nearby to mark the location. When we came upon it again, we slipped our packs off and searched the area, sweeping aside the mat-like cluster of junipers and kinnikinik (the dried leaves of which were used by the Indians as tobacco) to lay the ground bare.

In his rummaging John uncovered a horseshoe and called to me. While he cleaned it off with his bandanna I could hardly contain myself, thinking we'd unearthed an exciting piece of valley history. When he'd scraped off enough muck and rust to read the legend, John's face fell. "Made in Japan."

The shoe did, however, verify a story we had recently been told. The blazed trail had been used by an outfitter, years ago, to lead pack horses from the vicinity of Tungsten to Rabbitkettle Lake. The mystery of the blazes was solved.

All was well at the cabin when we arrived. A musty smell met our nostrils when we crawled through the trapdoor, but we soon aired the place out and had a fire going in the stove.

Before sitting down to study our maps, we set the spray cover, bailer, repair kit, paddles and trackline rope by the door.

*August 22nd*

Closing up camp has become a routine procedure for us. The cabin was locked up and the shutters refitted soon after breakfast. We headed west, under cloudy skies and a light drizzle. The Nahanni's level was lower than we had seen it, but the current was still strong. Instead of roaring from bank to bank, the silty water spiralled and foamed along exposed gravel beaches.

These bars were an advantage to us, because in tracking against the current we remained on shore to guide the canoe. We took turns pulling on the hundred-foot trackline attached to the bow and stern shackles, while we walked over the cobbled shoreline. The canoe had to be watched constantly to keep it in deep water and away from the rocks. By pulling in or slackening the trackline we could control the bow.

The width of the river varied — anywhere from twenty to sixty yards across — as did the amount of exposed shoreline. The river was not so co-operative as to allow us to stay on one shoreline the whole time. We tracked as far as we could on one side and then crossed to the opposite bank.

With every crossing we fell back a bit in the twelve-knot current, but the trick was not to lose too much ground.

In this current a straight paddling style was useless. We aligned the canoe at a forty-five degree angle to the current with the bow pointing to the opposite shore. Both of us paddled furiously on the downstream side while the current, running against the keel, forced the craft across the river.

More than once we missed our target altogether and found ourselves back at the bottom of the beach we had just tracked up! Our unfamiliarity with the river caused countless errors of judgement. Islands — some of them a quarter mile in length — posed the greatest problem, because we could not determine by any logical reasoning which side it would be possible to track up. Our choice was strictly hit and miss. Nine times out of ten, it seemed, we missed!

Our log for the day reads six miles, but this discounts the numerous times we retracked a section or were forced to choose another route. Whatever the distance, we were both sore and soaked to the skin from having to jump into waist-deep water and scramble to shore with the line when it looked as if we would miss our mark.

While one of us tracked, the other scavenged the beach for antlers or inspected the sand bars for animal prints. Of prime importance, though, was the task of scouting what lay ahead. Any decision about which side of the river was best for walking along was the sole responsibility of the scout. The person tracking had enough to think about keeping the loaded canoe out of the path of obstacles.

My respect for the early adventurers, who covered hundreds of miles in this manner, increased with every step.

By late in the day my ankles were so swollen and tender from stumbling over slippery rocks and hidden roots, that it was all I could do to ease my hiking boots off.

*August 23rd*

The going was slow around some islands upstream from our first camp, mostly due to our poor judgement of which side to track up. On two occasions we took the southern shore route, only to return downstream again and try the northern bank.

There were sections of the river where tracking beaches simply did not exist on either shore, nor a poling bottom, and we had to move upstream by pulling on the shoreline shrubbery. Progress was painfully slow and often it was halted completely by half submerged sweepers — fallen trees not completely uprooted from the bank, but whose branches extended out into the fast water several feet from shore. The method that worked best in these circumstances was to cut the branches off. Sitting on the bow deck with a swede saw, I removed the troublesome limbs while John steadied the craft and made sure the severed limbs floated well free of the canoe.

Past Bologna Creek, a little more than two miles from our cabin, the South Nahanni became virtually silt free. This tributary throws more granular sediment into the river than all the other feeder streams combined. The water was so clear that we could see the Arctic Grayling — a small grey-toned fish with a long flowing blue dorsal fin — milling about like herds where the streams poured into the main artery. Grayling rarely weigh more than four pounds but their numbers made up for any deficiency in size. Using our small spinners — the Mepp's Black Fury Number 1, the Mepp's Anglia Long and the Panther Martin spinner — we easily caught our limit of five a day.

*August 24th*

The sound of water splashing woke us. We bolted out of the tent expecting to see moose or caribou crossing the river, for there had been fresh tracks on the sand bar we were camped beside.

The noise came from a cliff disintegrating on the opposite shore. As the Nahanni swirled around the point of land we stood on, it rammed the full force of its current into the base of the sand and gravel cliff. Bit by bit the river was gouging the soft material away and every few minutes fragments would crash into the water.

The clatter of the sand hitting the water continued throughout breakfast and packing up. Just as we were making ready to leave, a lengthy flurry of splattering was followed by a tremendous roar — one gigantic piece of the escarpment leaned away from the face and tumbled into the water. The noise stunned us so that we just stood gawking at the hole left in the hundred-and-fifty-foot-high wall.

"I'm glad we weren't under that thing when it decided to go," I muttered to myself.

Once again we were witness to the power of the river. Slowly, over the decades, the South Nahanni would wear down the embankments that trapped it and carry the tons of gravel and soil elsewhere, only to grind it down again.

We were through the difficult stretches early in the day, so we took fishing breaks at every feeder stream. By dinner time five grayling lay in the bottom of the canoe, enough for dinner and the next day's breakfast.

We set up camp about two miles east of the Little Nahanni River, next to a bubbling creek. It was a lovely spot. The runoff in the creek chattered over the stones and emptied into the quieter South Nahanni. The beach we were camped on extended for a good half mile downriver. After dinner we walked along it, collecting driftwood for an evening campfire. The red glow of the sunset highlighted the uniform line of the spruce forest bordering the river. The low mountains to the north of us looked unreal in this twilight shadow. Instead of being rough and jagged like our home mountains, their soft folds and gentle curves made me think of sand dunes in a desert moulded by the force of the wind.

The sky was littered with stars and the moon was full. It was the first time we had really noticed them since coming to the valley. The spectacular display overhead and the silver beams of moonlight sparkling off the water made the perfect backdrop for our evening stroll.

"We've lived in this valley for over two months and this is the first night I haven't had the next day's plan mapped out in my mind. It feels nice," John sighed.

I can only compare my feelings of that moment to those I imagine older couples to feel about their retirement — a passage of time they can share intimately. Our homestead built, we had ahead of us ten glorious months to devote to one another. Already we realized we preferred working together, because it meant being vocal about our emotional and physical needs constantly.

"I'm, looking forward to what's in store for us." John slipped his hand in mine and squeezed it tightly.

"So am I, Joey."

*August 25th*

We had no idea what the temperature was but there was ice in the water pail and our J-cloth was stiff with frost at 8 a.m. Surely autumn days are just around the corner. The high cirrus clouds formed a wispy pattern in the morning sky while the sun shone bright but not yet warm. I could hardly wait to stand by the fire. Even in my sleeping bag I was chilled.

Breakfast was grayling fillets and Red River Cereal with coffee, piping hot, to warm our insides. We lingered around the fire longer than usual this morning, waiting for the sun to climb higher and thinking we should look for campsites that would get more early morning sun.

We planned to spend some time scouting the Little Nahanni, a major tributary, which we'd been interested in from the start of the trip. When we were travelling up the Alaska Highway, on the sunny days in late May, we talked of nothing else but canoeing the Little Nahanni River. That was how we originally planned to reach the Island Lakes. From reports we had read, the whitewater was superb, and the two-week trip would surely have been an exciting way to begin our year. But the spring thaw was late and the headwaters of the Little Nahanni were a block of ice when we arrived at Watson Lake. So it came to be that we flew in.

Sitting on the gravel bar we decided that a choice had to be made between the Little and South Nahanni Rivers. Which route to take? We couldn't make up our minds, so John scratched an S on one side of a stone and an L on the other.

Curiosity got the better of us when the South Nahanni won the first toss and we continued flipping, even though the lopsided pebble was heavily weighted in its favour. Oh well, we knew where we were headed. If the choice proved to be a poor one we could blame the stone.

The going was particularly rough, because the conifers hugged the shoreline. The maximum length of any one tracking beach was less than twenty yards. By dusk we were only two and a half miles above our noon stopover, our noses a little out of joint because we knew we had erred. The river was running very low here, and we had expected to see good tracking beaches, but they had dwindled out to nothing. The camping spots weren't much better. As we rounded each bend, I prayed for a level spot free of dense forest growth, to pitch the tent. But this wasn't to be.

In a last ditch effort to gain ground, we tried taking to the water ourselves and pulling the canoe, (a technique called frogging) but our attempts to fight the current, even close to shore were not successful. I was shivering after one plunge into the river and couldn't understand how John, who was soaked to the neck, was enduring the pain of the cold water.

*Joanne tracking the canoe*

"We can't go on like this much longer." I gasped.

"Its camp here I guess — or fall back downstream."

The decision was a tough one, but nightfall found us on the beach we had left that morning, glad to have seen at least a few more miles of the river, and accepting the fact that we'd probably come as far up the South Nahanni as we could.

*August 26th*

A day of rest seemed called for when the day broke fair and warm. We laid our ensolite pads on the sandy beach and read, while the sunshine soothed our stiff muscles.

Twice I thought I heard rustlings in the bush behind us. Each time I stiffened, sat upright and looked nervously behind, but saw nothing and returned to my book. But I was sure there was an animal lurking about, and I felt apprehensive about what I couldn't see.

"John, you hear anything?"

"No but you must. You're jumpy."

"This sounds silly but I'm sure there's some animal back there in the forest."

"You're right Jo. It does sound silly."

"Maybe its a bear!"

"So, he won't hurt us. Relax Jo."

John was right. At times my imagination gets the better of me and I worry too much about the animals' reactions to us. I want to believe that they're more frightened of us than we are of them — but the faith is weak. I wasn't aware of this fear until arriving in the valley. It surfaced the first night, when I imagined every animal within a ten-mile radius was seeking us out to get at our food.

"If we accomplish one thing over this year Jo, we're going to cure your animal phobia."

Well, I thought to myself, if I'm ever going to overcome it, this is the year.

*August 27th*

The temperature plunged during the night. I woke with the first light of dawn and was unable to fall back to sleep, so I implored John to rise with me. We got on the water early.

We drifted lazily downstream, with our fishing rods poised on the gunwales, hoping to entice the grayling with the small pieces of fin dangling from the end of our lures. After working so hard to get upriver, I felt deserving of this chance to sit back in my seat like a contented, overfed

*Grizzly tracks along the river bank*

tourist and do nothing more than ease my paddle into the river every once in awhile. We had to steer around rocks, but the current did the rest.

We had stopped at a creek to try a few casts when a movement from across the river caught my eye. A woodland caribou was standing at the water's edge. Without a word we pulled our lines in and paddled to the bottom of the rocky bar where the animal was drinking. He was a truly magnificent beast, his velvet covered antlers proudly displayed. He pranced towards us, his sharp hoofs clinking on the rocks, and then re-treated, only to reappear from behind a thicket of willows. Soon he would bound off again as if the devil were on his heels. It was rather like a game of hide and seek, but with John and me leaping from bush to bush at the same time, it was anyone's guess as to who was "it." John had the camera tucked under his arm, and when our inquisitive friend disappeared into a dense clump of alder and did not reappear right away, he slipped away to find better cover.

I stood by the canoe shouldering the .303 and for a moment considered using it. Just a fleeting thought, but for that fraction of a second I fell prey to the desire to secure a trophy. What restrained my trigger-happy urge was the sheer beauty of this animal, and the fear that I might miss the vital area and only wound him. If this admission qualifies me as a victim of buck fever, I accept the dishonour without argument. The "shots" John was taking were much more worthwhile.

We weren't far from home when we began thinking about the safety of the cabin and whether there had been visitors during our absence. Often we wondered about people's reactions to our presence in the valley. Would they feel that we had destroyed their wilderness experience by erecting a cabin on the shores of the river? We sincerely hoped not.

So far, we have had only one negative reaction to our presence and we never even saw our disgruntled visitors — a group known to us only by their rather colourful names: Muskeg, Jimbo, Sweet Miss Sue and Company.

They were close acquaintances of the "sweat lodge builders," who, before they left our site, asked us to store twelve litres of wine for Muskeg's crew. The two crews had arranged to cache the liquor supplies at the Moose Ponds, but the sweat lodge builders had run short of fuel and never made it to the headwaters of the South Nahanni. We had Muskeg's "load" and we were asked to pass it on. Weeks passed without our seeing Muskeg, and we began worrying for the safety of the party. Then, just days before our lengthy departure from the cabin we had a mail drop and the mystery was solved. A note informed us that Muskeg had paddled by our site early one morning, but refused to stop on the grounds that he dis-

*Woodland caribou*

liked people building cabins in the wilderness. We were free to use the wine as we saw fit.

*August 31st*
It feels good to be home again and into the routine of cutting and stacking firewood for the winter. Our daily quota of one cord a day provides us with just the right amount of exercise and fresh air, but still leaves us time to devote to other chores. Until now, we were using an open air kybo, but with cold weather coming even the thought is unbearable. It took us an afternoon to fell the trees needed for our small log privy. Around three sides of a six-foot-deep hole we notched and raised walls, leaving the fourth side open. We decided against hanging a door for two reasons: more air would circulate with a larger opening, and the distasteful job of keeping our privy cleaned out and deodorized, (with spruce boughs and ashes) would be easier if we had more elbow room. The structure only measured three feet square. The final touch was a flat roof stacked with as many sweet-smelling spruce boughs as we could fit on and pole supports for our toilet seat, which we could slide out of notches when it was necessary to clean out the pit.

When we were collecting roof poles for the privy we gathered extras, so we could build a canopy over the woodpile. This will help keep the snow off of our growing stacks of poplar and spruce.

On days when we feel unusually restless we go hiking. With the valley now wearing its cloak of autumn colours, there is no finer way to spend the time.

In a word, the fall landscape is stunning. The leaves on the birch and poplar are a rich golden yellow and the moss on the northern exposures to our south, a deep crimson. The colour changes are more pronounced the higher you climb. The waves of coniferous forests, showing no signs of colour change, just highlight the intensity of the newly clothed deciduous trees and the aqua-blue sparkle of the river, now running almost crystal clear. On the forest floor the small bushes and ground sweepers are splashed in warm sun shades.

The sun sets some two hours earlier than during the summer. Mornings are chilly and the person up first hustles into sweater, pants, and warm footwear to fill the wood box. With the cabin floor icy and the air so cold speed is essential.

I look forward to working outside. The aroma of wood smoke fills the clearing, and the special beauty of the mountains, alive in their kaleidoscope shades of orange, yellow and red, is with me daily.

*Snowshoe hare*

*The shy porcupine*

*September 4th*

An unexpected visitor lumbered down the path into camp shortly after dinner — the bulkiest porcupine we had ever set eyes on! When I first saw him I mistook him for a small black bear. The twilight of early evening was playing tricks on me.

He was one very frightened visitor. In the time it took me to drop the pails of water I carried, and to announce a newcomer in camp, he was up the nearest spruce and perched on the highest limb. There he remained, a huddled black ball, until well after midnight. When the light from our Coleman was out and the forest carried only the sounds of other wild creatures on the move, he departed.

*September 5th*

Just below our site, the South Nahanni splits into two channels around a large island and reunites about half a mile further downstream. A short distance beyond is a black sandy beach, pockmarked with the footprints of moose, bear, and wolves.

The water flowing from a narrow stream into the main channel of the Nahanni is warm here, with the nostril-constricting odour of sulphur. About a hundred yards off the river is the source of this tepid water. Hot-springs bubble out of the ground at temperatures as high as forty degrees Celsius.

John and I were enchanted with the vegetation surrounding the springs. Oversized clovers and large waxy-leaved plants gave the forest a tropical appearance. The large ferns climbed to our waists and juicy red raspberries were ours for the taking.

The greatest surprise was the meadow, where the springs bubbled up. Tall grasses and fireweed covered an area larger than a football field. The yellow poplar leaves quivered in the wind on the hillsides banking the area, and off to the north we could see the crest of a snow-capped range. Moose had rested in the tall grass, as the ground covering was well flattened in spots, and hoof marks covered the dark soil.

Enroute to the canoe, we uncovered parts of a flat bottomed scow, a rusty Coleman lantern, and a bullet-riddled tin of Roger's Golden Syrup. These discoveries touched off wild speculation.

"A scow. Now that dates back a ways. Albert Faille could have been..."

I laughed, because I was thinking exactly the same thing. The stories we had read about the Nahanni had highlighted the activities of this one man. As early as 1927, when Patterson spent his first summer on the river, he had travelled with a kicker-powered scow as far up the Nahanni as Virginia Falls. Faille's portage around the falls is still in use today. But complete details of what Faille did during his many years in this legendary wilderness, and in particular what country he saw above the falls, were not known to us.

We knew that Bill Addison, a native of Thunder Bay, Ontario, and a passionate lover of the northern wilderness, had been piecing together the history of the area through interviews with the old timers over the course of several summers. The material was in printed form at the Warden's Station in Nahanni Butte. We could hardly wait to get our hands on it! Until we did, though, we could only dream that the Nahanni's famous prospector-trapper had at one time roamed in what was now our home territory.

*September 7th*
The high bush cranberries have ripened in the valley and are ready for harvesting. The larger patches are in the more fertile areas, where the spring runoff caused some flooding. We pick pailfuls at a time, wash them thoroughly and then figure out what delectable recipe to try.

My northern cookbook lists page after page of cranberry recipes including breads, puddings, cakes, muffins, juice and sauce. They should last for a good part of the winter.

*September 8th*
Life is not dull by any standard definition of the word, but sometimes one of us wakes up with a restlessness that warns of the need for diversion. John has become good at detecting signs of this in my behaviour, even before I myself realize what is bothering me and why.

"You're not eating much. Something wrong?"

"I'm sick of the same old breakfast. I've no appetite."

The first time this happened, John didn't understand the symptoms. His lengthy, matter-of-fact reply that we just had to live with simple foods, that that was one of the sacrifices we had to make in order to live in isolation, and so on, was definitely not what I needed.

But one of John's strengths is his ability to learn from his errors. He soon switched to another approach. One that cured my fits of orneriness quite well.

"You're just bored with things generally. Let's eat breakfast and then take off for the day. A change of scene, okay? I need it too." This, spoken cheerfully and without condescension, worked wonders.

This morning we both woke feeling mildly lethargic and we recognized it in each other instantly.

*The Nahanni homestead*

"You feelin' down?"

"Yah, you too?"

"A little."

Good long talks help during mornings like this, not just to clear the air, but to convince us that we can work out emotional setbacks together. The old adage, "misery loves company" is appropriate here, in the sense that occasional feelings of depression are common to us both. I never feel alone when I'm down because I know John understands. Neither of us is of a morbid cast of mind, though. Having said what's bothering us we want to get on with cheering up.

Lately our pace has slowed a bit. I was conscious of this in myself and wanted to break out of the habit. Knowing how much John likes to go full tilt at a job I suggested that we choose a goal, like doubling or tripling our output of firewood for the day.

It worked too. We ended up with a huge pile of wood, and the satisfaction of going at the job until we were bone tired was like a shot of adrenalin.

Our time out of doors seems more important now that winter is drawing closer. Having only heard of temperatures of forty below, or even colder, there is a certain nervousness about actually experiencing them. Although the autumn colours remain on the slopes, the air carries a new briskness to it that speaks of the deep freeze ahead. Displays of the aurora borealis began tonight, another sign that winter isn't too far away.

We stumbled out of the cabin to witness the strange happenings in the sky. The night was pitch black, and we could see nothing but the long curtains of northern lights, tracing eery shadows across the darkness. It was as though a master switch controlled the draped bands of light, changing their intensity and direction constantly. What began as a single white streak in front of us grew brighter and larger. The most breathtaking moment occurred when another and then another band appeared, like corrugated, neon-bright sheets, twisting as they moved. Encircling us. I couldn't believe my eyes!

As soon as we went back inside the cabin we dove for the bookshelf. According to "The Northern Lights," an essay by B.W. Curries, published in *The Unbelievable Land*, we would not have proper radio communications during these light shows or for long periods afterwards. The electrons and protons that collide with the air molecules to cause the emissions of brightness also render the airways useless.

"Which means if an accident happens during the northern lights we can't get out on the radio for help," I said.

"Makes you feel isolated doesn't it?"

*The Northern Lights*

"Doesn't bother me, though."

Even when we bought the radio I liked to think of it as a means to talk with family every couple of months, not something to use so often that the sheer excitement of hearing their voices would be lost. Regular communication with other people would weaken the most important characteristic of our year — our being together and Really Alone!

# Cabin Life

The unused timber left lying around the forest in the wake of our tree fell-
ling exploits is now being cut into proper lengths to fit the firebox of our
stove. It is mostly spruce and poplar, in the early stages of drying out,
but usable, especially for all-night fires. A good slow ten-hour burn is
needed to maintain a comfortable temperature while we sleep —
comfortable being a few degrees above freezing. Driftwood and deadfall
are abundant, but when used alone they burn too hot and fast.

We are learning that different chores require specific types of fires.
Baking bread involves fiddling with the stove vents and amounts and
types of wood in order to get the oven up to the right temperature and
keep it there for two hours. Even the period beforehand, when the dough
is rising, is critical. Using a combination of bone dry and slightly green
wood produces the desired results, but there have been a few near catas-
trophes while learning the finer points. My first attempt at setting a morning fire forced John out of bed amidst clouds of suffocating smoke and
then, when cooking breakfast, I had the blaze so roaring hot I forced us
both out again, this time until the temperature in the cabin fell below the
thirty-five degrees Celsius registered on the thermometer.

With the cooler temperatures, it is quite safe and far more convenient
to store our food inside the cabin. Bulk storage bags of grains, cereals, canned goods, brown and white sugar, freeze-dried meats, desserts, spices,
and toiletries are kept on the rafters above the kitchen. The pails of margarine, jam, peanut butter, and cooking oil, along with boxes of raisins,
peanuts, dried fruit, powdered juices, and carob chips, are placed under
the bed, where the temperature is ten to fifteen degrees cooler.

This leaves the cache free for our winter meat (not yet taken) and our
survival gear. We have set aside a two-week supply of food, warm clothing, fuel, a small stove, and a tent in case the cabin should burn down — a
horrible thought but one we have to consider. To these emergency provi-

sions have been added two pairs of crude plywood snowshoes, in the event that our webbed ones are destroyed. As simple as these are, we could make the distance to Tungsten on them.

The thought of facing a severe northern winter unprepared was the impetus for undertaking many small chores around the cabin. We have scrupulously checked every seam in the cabin walls. Wherever we felt air seeping through spaces between the logs, we restuffed the cracks with handfuls of moss, then drove the chinking in using a hammer and wedge.

We have also cut a second front door and installed it over the original, hoping that this will minimize the draft.

*September 10th*

We received a radio call just before dinner that struck us dumb. A close friend of ours is flying in for a week-long visit.

The minute we completed the call with Doug we began a round of frenzied activity. There were hangers to make, along with a third chair, and the cabin had to be spruced up to accommodate another person. Because we did not know his exact arrival time we worked all the harder.

This waiting period was the first time that we felt the distance between ourselves and family. It would take Doug almost a day of flying to get to our location, and given the northern approach to life generally, he was apt to spend a couple of days in Watson Lake arranging for a Cessna for the last leg of the journey.

We hoped he would make it in before the fall colours faded. Already the crimson shades of moss were turning a rustic amber and the golden poplar leaves, so lovely against the dark spruce, were drifting to the ground. We wanted so badly to have him view the valley in its autumn glory, but each day that passed greatly reduced our chances of sharing it with him.

*September 15th*

We have been searching the sky for days. By late afternoon today we were ready to abandon the vigil when the drone of a small plane coming through Bologna Creek Pass sent us scuttling down to the river bank. We had been told that the river was too shallow and swift in front of our home to attempt a float landing, but the pilot splashed down right in front of us, giving Doug a sensational introduction to northern life and almost giving us heart attacks.

Poor Doug. He was smothered with our exuberant embraces and so many questions in the first few minutes that he had no chance to ask any of his own. "What was the flight like?" "Did you have any trouble booking the Cessna from Watson? "How long can you stay?" All questions that could wait, but like two curious children our tongues were going at full throttle.

Until his arrival on the South Nahanni, Doug had been sharing our bush life vicariously through our correspondence. Now he was eager to see everything first hand. Once his baggage was unloaded he surveyed the clearing from the end of the rocky bar. Much of what he looked at had been so graphically described in letters it didn't take him long to get oriented.

"Let's see this cabin up close. Boy, you two did a great job! It looks terrific!"

While telling us about the trip from Toronto and passing on greetings from mutual friends, he rummaged through bags and packs for the special foods, pictures, and letters he had brought.

Over a barbeque dinner (oh, those mouth watering cheeseburgers) we all began to settle down. The week ahead, we promised him, would be unmitigated bliss — a chance for us to do more than just talk about the good life. He wanted to see, and we wanted to show him, every foot of the countryside we called home.

*September 18th*

Doug's enthusiasm for the valley and the animal life made John and me nostalgic as we recalled our feelings during the first weeks of our stay. Our hardy companion enjoyed the wilderness as much as we did, and his eagerness to share some of our experiences pleased us greatly. The more he saw, the more Doug understood our love for the valley.

We were a compatible threesome, enjoying the camaraderie of the trail and the confidences we shared around the kitchen table — and on this morning, a good laugh too.

"Jo, do you mind if I pull these bedroom curtains closed to keep the sun out of my eyes?" Doug asked me. Before I could explain that he'd have a little trouble doing that, he was out of his sleeping bag and yanking at the material.

My face was scarlet with embarrassment. Fighting the urge to fall to the floor in a fit of giggling, I went over to the window and pointed to the two screw nails that attached half the curtain to the log wall.

"It's for show, Doug. These curtains wouldn't budge if you tried."

Now Doug was embarrassed, but he recovered like a pro. Some

lighthearted remark was made about the disadvantages of having an inquisitive houseguest, and the matter was dropped. The more I thought of it though, the funnier the incident seemed. For the rest of the day I kept seeing the look on Doug's face, so puzzled when he couldn't get the curtain to move and so shocked when he realized why.

### September 21st

The week has passed all too quickly. Doug leaves tomorrow. A full day of flying will see him home by Saturday night and allow him some mental recuperation time to prepare for Monday and his hectic business life in Toronto.

We were in the midst of a celebration dinner and decked out in our finest when Gene, the helicopter pilot for a nearby mining camp, dropped us off two desperate guests. Welcome North Mines had set up its exploration camp about two miles west of us in early August and was planning to close up the operation within a few days.

As we heard it, Kip and Julian were trippers who had landed at the Moose Ponds earlier in the month, not knowing the water level in the upper reaches of the South Nahanni is so low at this time of year as to make navigation almost impossible. Whether these men were forewarned of this and chose to ignore good advice or never thought to inquire we did not know.

For almost two weeks the pair had dragged and lugged their canoe nearly sixty miles, using all but a small portion of the rations that were meant to carry them through to Nahanni Butte. Fortunately for them they were rescued by Gene earlier in the day and taken to the mining camp.

Kip and Julian lasted one hour in the camp before the cook decided she had had enough. She was frightened to death of the large hunting knives dangling from the leather pouches around their waists. Kip's incessant chatter about his oneness with wolves and his war experiences did nothing to increase his popularity in camp.

We had spoken to Gene earlier in the day so he knew of Doug's intention to fly home. He also knew we owned a radio and could make arrangements for a larger plane to fly in and take all three men to Watson Lake. When the presence of these men became too much, he wasted little time ferrying them into our camp.

John, Doug and I had so wanted to have this last evening to ourselves, but we recovered from the intrusion without showing our disappointment. The men were clearly in need of food and some cheering up. Dinner was postponed until plans to charter a larger plane were confirmed and our overnight guests settled in.

*September 22nd*
Clouds rolled in during the night and by morning any hopes of flying out were dashed. Our trio of guests was laid over for another day.

Veteran travellers in the North are quite accustomed to such occurrences; in fact Doug had made allowances for bad weather and told his secretary he might be behind schedule. Our other two visitors felt they had endured quite enough misfortune for one trip, and they found the delay unfathomable. When the cloud cover began to lift they were convinced the plane would show; when it didn't they were even more depressed and disappointed. They were impervious to any explanation, and the seeds of discontent were sown.

*September 23rd*
The first layover day was a long and disconcerting one. The hopeful expressions of Kip and Julian faded into silent aggravation by nightfall, when it was obvious that no plane was coming. Today, the pattern repeated itself. We awoke to a low ceiling of fog, gloomy rain-bearing clouds, and no radio communication. Weather conditions did improve slightly, later in the day, but this only provoked more disgruntled comments from our newest boarders.

*September 24th*
Tempers were reaching such a volatile state that something had to be done. Radio communications were out again and it was anyone's guess if or when a plane would arrive. To top it off, snow had fallen above treeline and the surrounding mountains wore a veil of mist and fog.

Doug, seemingly unaffected by the delay, remarked that if he had to be stuck somewhere he couldn't have chosen a nicer spot. His flippant suggestion that they get a second cabin underway, to shelter them for the cold winter months ahead, was met with hostile stares from Kip and Julian.

I was purposely throwing myself into menial kitchen chores as this discussion continued and John, I noticed, was nonchalantly removing the clip from the .303 on the wall. I felt sure that if the plane didn't come soon, someone would explode.

John drew me to one side of the kitchen to tell me about Kip's knife-throwing antics (he had almost severed the counterweight from the aerial hookup outside). This didn't bother me as much as the knife itself. I was beginning to sympathize with Welcome North's camp cook.

What grated on my nerves even more was Kip's high-pitched, almost hysterical laugh. He seemed always on the brink of being completely out of control, and this sent chills up my spine. Whenever possible I tried to put distance between him and myself. Julian spent most of his time sulking like a wounded pup. I'd never seen such a chronic case of depression.

In an attempt to defuse the situation John announced that we were all going to work — to construct a cache.

"And then we're going to fill it with moosemeat." he stated emphatically.

The work seemed to ease tensions slightly, but dissension arose when Kip objected to killing the moose. An uncomfortable silence fell over the group.

My own decision in favour of the moose hunt had been made with considerable apprehension, but only because we did not have a license yet. We had been feeding our hungry guests for three days and if they were stuck here much longer our own rationing would get tighter. So far, the only dent being made was in such precious commodities as coffee, sugar and margarine — despite our telling Kip and Julian of the amount allowed each person. Julian's retort to my reminders to go easy on these had been an offhand, "Don't worry, when I get out of here, I'll send some in to you."

My inner restraint wavered further when I discovered that our year's supply of jelly beans and ju-jubes (a gift from Doug) was missing, and it was all I could do to keep the incident to myself. I knew I needed time to contemplate the proper limits of northern hospitality under such circumstances, before I dared relay the news to John.

I was spared confrontation by the sputtering of an engine overhead. At last! The Beaver had arrived! There were expressions of relief all around.

Doug boarded the plane with the others, but not without first sharing a private chuckle with us. "I'll write you a long letter. This has been some vacation!" he laughed. Before the Beaver taxied down the river to prepare for liftoff he shouted from the front window, "The life of one moose was saved today."

Standing beside me on shore, John muttered: "Those two in the backseat are lucky their tickets arrived this afternoon too!"

*September 26th*

Life isn't quite the same since Doug left. We find ourselves reliving the events of his visit, especially the Kip and Julian episode. As strained as the atmosphere was during that three day period, it is amusing in retrospect.

We were again settling back into the peacefulness of cabin life when Lou, Chief Park Warden for Nahanni National Park, paid us a visit. There was an epilogue to the drama of the lost travellers, and that was the reason for his presence.

For every traveller on the river, Lou had a tentative trip itinerary. When canoeists do not show up at Nahanni Butte near the date they have indicated or notify the authorities of a change in their planned schedule, a search party is organized. The search for Kip and Julian was in its second day!

As we recounted the events of their stay, Lou's expression changed from concern for the two to controlled anger. And he had every right to feel as he did, given the cost of helicopter time. We assured him that had our radio been operating we would have called to inform his office of the outcome; but, of course, this was no consolation — the damage was done!

Lou also delivered a letter to us from our mentor, R.M. Patterson. The author who had first inspired us to homestead on the South Nahanni River had this to say:

August 21, 1978

Dear Mr. and Mrs. Moore

Thank you for your letter and I was interested to hear of your plans. You do not say where on the river you are building your cabin and I was at a loss to figure out the location, all the names being new since 1927-28 — unless the place is in the Splits opposite the Twisted Mountain and close to what we called Jackfish Lake — now, on the map, Yohin Lake? The area can be wet enough to call marsh.

Thank you for the invitation but I probably shall not be in the Nahanni area again. (a) I saw it untouched and at its best through three perfect summers. I could never improve on that, and (b) all the people I knew there have moved away or died. Of the five men who were on the river in '28-29, only Stevens and I remain: he at Yellowknife and I here (or off on some trip).

And with increasing age one's interests change. One may be no longer able to climb mountains and bash around in the bush, but that does not prevent a man from being interested in other things, involving perhaps a trip to Scotland, France, Spain — somewhere where the trails have been cut out and improved upon over the centuries and where, except after storm, one is unlikely to find the trail blocked by fallen timber.

Well — have a good winter and not one like the winter I clicked for — the deepest snow in many years and then break trail on snowshoes down the Liard to Simpson.*

All the best, from
R.M. Patterson.

*September 28th*
The light drizzle that fell during the last days of Doug's visit dropped snow on the alpine meadows. Ice forms each night between the rocky crevices on the shoreline, while more permanent layers have stilled the waters in the river's snyes. The leaves have begun to fall. Even the slightest breeze shakes the stands of birch and alder, causing the frost-tipped leaves to drift down into windrows in each clearing. As the days roll by more of the autumn colours are disappearing.

Mornings are misty and grey, with low clouds hanging like shrouds over the valley. Late afternoon showers are the order of the day and at night we fall asleep to the dull thud of raindrops on the sod roof. We are enveloped by cloud constantly, a bleak outlook if winter is going to bring the same. Even the warmth of the cabin, with its cosy, cheerful interior, is little solace. Books and projects satisfy us for a time, but it is the outdoors and the relaxed feeling of being well exercised that we miss.

It has become necessary to ignore the foul weather altogether. Clad in our bright red ponchos and rain chaps we walk along the gravel bars, fish, collect driftwood, or sit by an outdoor fire with stiff hands clutched around a hot drink. We simply were not born to sit idle inside all day and for our mental and physical welfare we try to not even acknowledge the dampness, or the gray haze along the shoreline where the birch and poplars stand, stripped bare.

We dress for the rain, make note of it in the diary, and then ignore it. It is the only way!

*September 29th*
The neighborhood populace of whiskey jacks has taken to congregating around us, no matter if we are in the woods or near the cabin, so we decid-

---

* Patterson is referring here to a gruelling snowshoe trip he made in midwinter from his cabin in Deadmen Valley to Fort Simpson, N.W.T.

ed to build them a feeder. They scrutinized the entire operation from their spruce bough perches while we sank a post into the ground and set a small station on top. I set patties of Red River Cereal and bacon fat on the tray — our only choice of feed — and then we left them to poke around while we cut up lengths of driftwood from a large pile across the river.

There wasn't a winged visitor in sight when we returned for lunch, and it didn't take long to discover why. While we watched from the kitchen window, the marten tramped noisily around the station. Tin had been nailed around the post, so his attempts to climb up failed miserably. He scrambled up a nearby spruce, and like a leopard hawk ready to pounce on his prey, eyed the feed.

"He's going to take a flying leap at the station," John exclaimed.

Instead he descended and leapt easily from the ground onto the feeder, then devoured every crumb on the tray. No wonder the grey jays weren't using the station — it wasn't safe.

*September 30th*

The day started out smoothly enough. I was up first to refill the firebox while John smothered his face in a pillow trying to stifle the urge to correct my unorthodox (or so he said) fire starting techniques. I ignored him and continued laying the split pieces of dry wood on top of the bed of twigs and paper. The fire lit, I donned my usual multiple layers of clothing while huddling as close to the stove as I dared. Meanwhile John tore around the kitchen like a human cyclone, heaving boxes out of the rafters and flipping the lids carelessly off the tins on the counter, trying to find the missing ingredients he sought for breakfast preparation.

We were beginning our "new routine" for kitchen duties — another strategy to fight cabin fever. The boredom problem was spreading into other areas. Small idiosyncrasies we each had were beginning to loom large — a dangerous situation when you haven't a place to retreat to if an argument over some triviality erupts. We hoped the change of routine would combat this, and so the responsibility of chef had passed to John, while I took over clean-up duties.

Morning coffee was served à la chef Moore — a delightful recipe of brewed coffee spiced with cinnamon — and breakfast followed soon after. When I rose from my chair to help bring the food and dishes to the table John stopped me.

"I'm the cook Jo. You just relax!"

Not wanting to stir up any trouble but thinking to myself that we might be carrying this "role" business a bit too far, I reluctantly sat down and

*A marten getting his share of moosemeat*

*An overfed grey jay*

stayed quiet while John ran his shuttle service between stove, counter, and table.

I ended up feeling like a guest in my own home; John couldn't eat with me — there wasn't time! He was trying to serve all the dishes at once, and he no sooner started to eat than he realized the jam and margarine were missing and was up to get them.

"Those small containers have to be refilled. We finished up our week's ration of both jam and margarine last night," I explained a little sheepishly.

With one long groan of displeasure, John pulled out the thirty-pound plastic pails from under the bed, and using our spatula, divvied out a serving. Then back he came to the table to eat his now cold plate of cheese omelette.

"My toast!" he shrieked.

In the frying pan on the stove were his four slabs of bread, charcoal black on the underside. He'd forgotten to flip them over.

I had enjoyed my breakfast, but the same could hardly be said for the cabin's new chef.

The kitchen was in complete disarray, with half-open boxes everywhere and the pile of dishes left for the dishwasher — me — to clear away. I tackled the mess silently, but inwardly my blood pressure was rising.

One of my bad habits was using every dish in the house at mealtime and leaving a monstrous pile for John to wash. For every recipe I concocted, I used far too many pots, pans, saucers, and worst of all, utensils. But I was attempting to kick the habit and recently had noticed an improvement in the size of the dish pile. I thought John must have been in a cranky mood the night before when, in the middle of cleanup, he announced that he had had it with dirty dishes! The incident prompted the discussion that ended with our decision to change roles. Now, as I cleaned up, I counted all but three dishes dirty. It was revenge he was after!

It was too early to discuss the matter. One of the things we agreed upon when deciding on our new routine was to hold off voicing our feelings about how we liked or disliked it until midweek. That way we could break into our new roles slowly, maybe even try out some fresh ideas.

If breakfast was bad, no words can describe the dinner hour. The culinary arts involve far too much waiting around, timing, fiddling with the stove to get proper heat, and battling with recipe cards to suit John. He was not only weak from hunger by the time dinner was served, he was tied up in knots.

After dinner every dish in the house was dirty. I finished the cleanup without saying a word and we went our separate ways.

My face was buried in a book, but more to hide my glum expression than from interest. I was angry over the issue of the dirty dish pile, because I felt I had been had. But it really was such a trivial thing. Why couldn't I just blurt out that I thought it unfair of him to create such a mess in the kitchen when all along he'd been complaining about my doing it? No, I wasn't in control yet. I'd probably light into him and then feel sorry later that I'd spoken too harshly. I can wait, I thought, until the air clears a bit.

But it wasn't getting better. Hours ticked away with nothing said. The cabin was like a tomb.

I was beginning to question our ability to restore the strained atmosphere to some level of normalcy. How had such a minor issue developed into this?

Instead of ridding my thoughts of what had transpired I began to feel sick from thinking about it too much. I wasn't sure that John was purposely ignoring me until he got up to make himself a coffee and didn't offer me one; then I knew we were having a fight.

"He can't sit in that chair all night," I thought. Sooner or later this had to come to a head. Better now than later.

"You want to talk?" I asked meekly.

"What's there to talk about? You've been mad at me since breakfast. You don't even have to say anything any more. I know!"

"It isn't all my fault."

"You started it."

"No one started it!" I shouted.

Before John could yell back I continued — trying to speak calmly.

"Look, I'm not blaming you, but something's bothering me. Can I tell you what it is?"

"Please do."

"Why did you use every dish in the house for breakfast and dinner when you've been telling me I shouldn't?"

"So that's what's wrong. Well I didn't do it intentionally."

"Can you understand how I might have misinterpreted it though?"

"Yeah, I guess so."

"Can we go back to our old routine?" I said, almost pleadingly.

John came over and sat on the bed beside me. "Sure I hate cooking more than I do cleaning up!"

The quick end to the argument was as startling as its beginning. It showed us — at least I hope it did — that even newlyweds can't let disagreements simmer when they're living in such close quarters. Not only is it vital to speak up as soon as a troublesome situation arises, but somehow we have to maintain our individuality and separate opinions.

*October 1st*

A low ceiling of threatening clouds and a cool five degrees greeted us this morning, but the gloom couldn't keep us indoors. After eggs and toast, and our usual overindulgence in coffee, we canoed to the opposite shore.

The last few weeks had found us so involved in preparations for winter we hadn't noticed the furious activity going on in the forest. Chipmunks and red squirrels their jowls bulging with nuts, raced along the paths to their storage dens. The snowshoe hares thumped over the ground cover of dried leaves, stopping only long enough to sniff at the base of trees and bushes before leaping into action again. The gray jays, who stay put for the winter, unlike the ducks and geese, were also foraging for food.

The sight of a black wedge of geese embossed on the slate grey sky, and the sound of their migration chant, made me lonesome for the warmer weather. For that brief moment I longed for a return of colour to the forest and the long days of summer. Now the only colour was at our feet, where piles of decaying leaves were scattered, their musty aroma rising to meet our nostrils.

The game trails we used as footpaths branched off in all directions. Some crossed each other at right angles, giving the impression of walking beside blocks of carefully manicured gardens. The pillows of moss, covering mounds of earth and leaves, looked like separate plots of land, divided by the trenches of well-used trails. The soft green of lichens, the faded golds and oranges of poplar leaves, the wispy ferns, and the creeper bushes — some bearing fruit — seemed deliberately patterned to brighten the forest floor. We were photographing these natural floral arrangements when a loud crack, followed by a thud, sent a tremor through the forest.

"Beavers," John whispered.

He broke into a cautious run, with me close at his heels. We headed towards the river bank, downwind of a grove of poplar trees we had spotted earlier in the morning. It was from here that we assumed the noise must have come — the site where two beavers were felling trees to use in the building of their dam and lodge.

We took to all fours, to crawl more stealthily through the buckbrush, until we came within sight of the clearing. A number of poplars were downed, some stripped of their branches completely, so we concealed ourselves in a shallow pit, screened in on three sides by dense alder growth, and waited.

Our approach had been well timed. No sooner were we behind cover than we saw the sleek head of a beaver break the surface of the water close to the bank. We watched while the black body waddled onto land towards a fallen poplar and gnawed off a limb. But instead of swimming upriver to return to his lodge, he continued overland with a mouthful of poplar trailing to one side.

Before the industrious little fellow disappeared down the skidway that led to the house, I caught a glimpse of his hindquarters. I was fascinated at the texture of the tail. Hairless, it resembled an oversized human tongue in the later stages of rigor mortis.

The beaver seemed to drag this appendage behind him as he walked, but I wasn't close enough to tell whether it was only slightly lifted or left to hang limp. During the hour we remained in our cubbyhole, the beaver returned twice more to chew off a limb and carry it home.

Later, on examining the tracks, we found that most had been wiped out — either by the broom-like poplar branch or the beaver's substantial tail.

*October 3rd*
In the early hours a light showering of snow flakes swept over the clearing, and when we woke, it was to a pure white and serene world.

*October 4th*
The moose are now roaming the valley floor in a state of utter confusion. It is rutting time, when the overwhelming desire to reproduce plays havoc with their usually unaggressive natures. From what we've read, they stop eating at this time while the bulls engage in an almost continuous round of head-on battles, day and night.

This afternoon, when working alone in the kitchen while John was off fishing, I was halted by an uncomfortable feeling of being watched. I looked up, expecting to see John dangling another gigantic Dolly Varden in front of me, but was taken aback a see a moose peering in the window. His enormous head filled the window frame, and his large snout was pressed against the pane.

The sight of the forlorn creature sent a wave of pity through me. "You poor confused beast," I giggled to myself. "You don't know enough to be afraid of me." I contemplated opening the door but common sense steered me from that course. Moose in rut are very unpredictable creatures, and not all as docile as this one.

This afternoon we got the scare of our lives. I was slightly indisposed when we heard the unearthly bellowing and crashing outside the bedroom window. I had one leg into and the other out of a pair of jeans, but the sight of two enraged bulls charging straight at the cabin hastened the dressing process.

The bedevilled hulks were racing down the game trail, their faces locked in concentration. They were headed straight for us.

"They're going to ram right into the window!" I croaked. One look at the twisted branches and flattened bushes in the wake of their fury was enough to convince me that nothing could stop them.

In the split second it took to realize the danger we were in, we had thrown ourselves onto the bed. Then suddenly, only feet away from the window, the lead bull veered north and the second followed — taking the right angle turn so sharply it was a wonder they stayed on their feet.

We rushed outside but the pair were long gone. We could hear the snap of branches and the animals' snorts and grunts as they levelled everything in their path.

*October 9th*

When the clouds broke enough to reveal the sun, we were reminded that our chief source of light was sinking rapidly out of view. It no longer travels high above the range of mountains to our south, but skirts behind them, backlighting each peak in a halo of golden light. It appears in a bright splash of brilliance for short periods that are becoming more infrequent. It will only be a matter of days before it fades out of sight completely.

*October 13th*

More snow fell overnight, which means that the canoe must soon be staged for the winter. But before flipping it over onto the poles we have lashed between four poplars, we tracked upstream a short way for our final river run of the season. Huge flakes fell softly to the ground around us and dissolved on touching the South Nahanni's frigid waters. The river was running some slush on our return home, and by nightfall there was a solid sheet of ice along the shoreline. Temperatures are one and two degrees below freezing now — day and night.

*October 14th*

We had talked for weeks of reorganizing the rafters so we could find things more easily, and when the day greeted us with snow flurries and gloomy skies, we decided to do it.

Every item we have in stock (and, thanks to Doug, this includes another eighty-eight pounds of white flour) was itemized, repacked, and stored in monthly allowances. Everything from toilet paper and soap to our special foods was quantity controlled more strigently than ever before. In the summer months, especially during our eighteen-hour building days, we had been lax about desserts and the number of loaves of bread we ate in a week.

Fuel was calculated to the last ounce for lantern efficiency. We now live by the chart on the wall that outlines how many hours of lantern time we can afford — and for mid-October this means five hours of light per day. We jokingly refer to our time zone as CST — Coleman Saving Time. An extra hour will be added each week until January, when we will begin decreasing the time.

*October 19th*

John was up first. I heard him crawl out of bed and stumble into shirt and pants while he delivered a brief address on the less appealing features of our outdoor privy.

"Do me a favour will you, Jo. Don't let me drink even an ounce of liquid after dinner. This getting up at dawn is madness! It's cold out there. And that blasted toilet seat — it's freezing! I'm bringin' that thing in from now on." Once collected, he forced himself out the door to brave the cold morning.

I buried myself deeper under two layers of down, hoping my beloved spouse would see to the fire when he returned. The morning stroll usually sparked life into the unfortunate who was forced out of bed first by the call of nature.

There was no drag in John's footsteps when he returned.

"Jo! Wake-up!" he yelled. "The moose is back and he's eating."

This was news! For three consecutive mornings we had not seen our two neighbourhood moose. The fact that this fellow outside was nibbling on bushes meant that he was out of rut. His meat would no longer be tainted, and if we wanted winter meat, this was the time to take it.

The consultation was brief. Our big game license had been approved, so we were entitled to the animal under the law. The recent food check showed the need for meat, and the day was tolerable enough for the skinning and gutting process.

I wished John luck as he took the Lee Enfield off its rack, and prayed inwardly that it would go well. This was his first hunt ever, and because it was more out of need than desire, it would most likely be his last. I sensed he wanted it done quickly.

The moose was still standing out front, only fifty or so yards from where John knelt and braced his firing arm against the picnic table. The hefty bull chomped away on the alders, oblivious to the scheme underway to end his life. John fired.

The moose did not drop as I thought it would. Instead, it broke into a run. John made a move to follow, but then stopped and fired two more shots.

The door flew open with such a racket I though John was trying to kick it in. He was confused and angry by the look of his furrowed brow and blazing eyes. His breaths were coming in short gasps.

"I just wounded him. The sights were set wrong. I only had three bullets."

There was no point in asking questions; every minute wasted meant the bull would be farther away. "He's gone into the bush," John said. "I'll try to follow his tracks.

I was as frantic as John, worried for his safety and hoping that the moose was not suffering unduly. "Be careful!" I urged as he grabbed a handful of bullets from a box, shoved them into the clip one at a time and tore out the door.

A loud "pop" resonated from the forest and, only minutes later, John returned.

"If you can call taking a moose on your front lawn a hunt, then the hunt is over." he mumbled as he sank into the chair. After collecting himself he blurted out the story as though making a confession.

"He hadn't gone far when I picked up his trail. One of the first three shots must have caught him in the lower chest. Anyway, it slowed him down and left a trail of blood in the snow. And I could smell him. I was afraid he might charge at me if I cornered him — you know how dense those birch and spruce are behind the cabin. I found him in a small clearing and got within thirty feet, but I stayed next to a good sized spruce. If he moved, I was going to climb it. He looked pretty miserable — the only problem was, he insisted on looking the other way and after my first three mistakes, I was eager to finish him off right. So I kind of groaned and he turned towards me. One shot between the eyes and he collapsed."

"This is our bible for today," I said, as I produced *The Handy Guide for Dressing Big Game*. We skipped breakfast and, equipped with newly sharpened swiss army knives, an axe, and a saw, hurried back to the spot where the moose lay. Step by gory step we followed the rules set out in the handbook — from bleeding the carcass, to skinning and cutting it up. The instructions, although straightforward and simple in theory, were gruesome in practice. But we managed, together, to finish the job, and by dinnertime the hind and front quarters and both sets of ribs were on drainage racks in the cache. The liver and brains we took home with us.

Three holes filled with leftovers and covered with shovelfuls of earth were the property of four whiskey jacks. They feasted like gluttons on whatever they could find. It was not long before the ravens joined them; they had been perched on the tree tops all day surveying the scene and cawing fiercely.

The final cleanup meant dragging the pungent, bloodstained hide to the riverbank where we left it to drain and air out on the rocks.

*October 21st*
Winter has ceased her false accusations. The temperature never rises now above five below and the blustery wet snows have given way to light fluffy flakes that stay with us. Snowshoes and skis are already necessary for outdoor mobility, but we no longer have the sun to encourage us. At noon today we bid our fiery companion farewell. She crept from behind the Three Bears, poured her golden rays on the cabin, the frosted trees, and our uplifted faces. For all of one minute she blazed out of a blue sky unbroken by cloud, and then she was gone.

*October 22nd*
Evicting the assemblage of wayward field mice who sought shelter in our cabin for the winter — and a free meal from the bags of freeze-dried food stored on the bottom kitchen counter — brought on no feelings of remorse. If anything, filling the traps with a much rationed supply of cheese proved to be more painful. But at last the cabin was restored to our occupancy only.

*October 27th*
We left the cabin shortly after breakfast for a ski run on Snake Creek, now a frozen highway. Along the path heading north we were halted in our tracks by a commotion in a treed area near where the moose carcass was buried. The rustling sound we heard was fading rapidly, so we quickened our pace, intending to catch a glimpse of the animal, who evidently feared us.

Our intruder was a bear, sporting a black shiny coat and layer on layer of rippling fat. What a creature he was, lumbering along at a fast clip without so much as breaking stride to look back at us. The man smell must have startled him, for he moved with great purpose, his sole objective, it seemed, to reach the safety of his den on the double.

I was glad to see the bruin making a hasty exit. His nervous reaction to our presence helped stifle my fear.

Such encounters still make me edgy, and it was a few minutes before I responded to John's prodding to continue our ski. My knees were wobbly, but I began to see the humour in the episode.

"He sure burned the calories on that retreat," I chuckled. John, knowing how uncomfortable I was after such events, remarked that my laughing about it was a reassuring sign.

*John carving steaks off the moose carcass*

We had only skied another hundred yards or so when John turned abruptly and motioned me to stop. He didn't have to say a word — I could see for myself we weren't alone on the path. Just ahead of us was a wolf.

He was partially hidden by the tall grasses along the arm of Snake Creek, carefully picking his way through the snow. It did not appear that he was travelling in any particular direction, just investigating the frozen ground and trying to gain a proper foothold. Then, in one great leap, he landed on the ice, made less slippery by the frosting of new snow, and broke into a run.

I was struck with wonder at the size and stature of this animal. Having never seen wolves before, I had imagined them to look like large dogs, but this wild creature was heavy set — my guess was that he weighed more than a hundred pounds — and his colouring was not what I expected either. He looked as though a bottle of peroxide had spilled across his back, bleaching parts of his black and grey coat.

My reaction was absolute fear when he darted out of cover and, for an instant, seemed to be heading our way. I slid closer to John, who was so awed by the sight that he too was frozen in his tracks.

Without a warning at all, the wolf slid back on his haunches, raised his head to the sky and let out a high pitched howl. And boy, did he get an answer! The chorus of yelps and howls that followed in response to his salute is a sound I shall never forget.

"There must be hundreds of them," John exclaimed. Hundreds indeed! There was an army of wolves emerging from the forest and screaming at us. I was so frightened I just wanted to flee to the cabin, hoping John would come to his senses and follow suit.

"Jo! Wait! They're not going to hurt us."

"That's no welcoming committee in front of us. Count them! I see over thirty. Look, they're scaring me to death. Please let's go home."

"But Jo, I've got the gun. Trust me, it's okay. Now we came here to ski. Are you going to let these fellows scare you?"

I'm sure it was written all over my face — the answer was yes. With only eight shells in the Lee Enfield and my recount turning up more than three dozen wolves less than fifty yards from us, I was convinced our end was near. I wanted so badly to turn and go home but John wouldn't budge. It was his final argument that persuaded me to follow.

"Jo," and he spoke softly and confidently, "the Sierra Club offered ten thousand dollars to anyone who could relate an authentic story of a wolf attacking a man. To this day, no one has collected the money.

Shaken and almost sick, I waited with John to observe the workings of the pack. Call it what you will, but if he was stubborn enough to stay put with thirty-eight (final count) wolves in full view, I wasn't leaving him to do it alone. If he was going to risk their attacking him then I was standing my ground too. That much I believed in.

The nerve-frazzling chorus ceased and the pack disbanded. Each wolf — and they were an assortment of every size and colour — could see and smell us, and while some held their ground and peered suspiciously at us, others followed a large, jet black wolf up the height of land to the north. One by one they scampered up the slope and disappeared.

"They're heading out." I whispered.

"Then let's ski!"

We moved slowly forward, eyes riveted on two straggling wolves who remained behind the rest. Their actions were in accord with much that is written about the highly organized behaviour of large packs. These two were the rear guards, and not until every wolf was out of sight did they too climb the hill.

The nervous energy that had welled inside me as we waited for the lead wolf to make his move was converted to more constructive purposes. I skied for hours up and down Snake Creek, releasing every ounce of adrenalin that poured through my veins. When we returned to the cabin late that afternoon, I was as calm as when I had first strapped on my skis.

*November 1st*

It was well past darkness when we heard shuffling noises outside and the sound of metal clanging against metal. John grabbed the lantern from its hook and shone it out the front window while I peered into the darkness from the kitchen window, thinking I might see the animal retreat. There was no sign of activity.

"I don't hear him," John said in a low voice. "He's probably taken off in another direction."

Slowly I opened the front door while John shone the light onto the picnic table and the snow covered ground around it. Still no signs of movement.

"I hear something near the canoe." I exclaimed.

We hurried outside, John waving the lantern to and fro to illuminate the patches of darkness. Suddenly a round black ball emerged from under the staged canoe and scurried toward the rocky bar. It was gone in a flash.

"Too fast for a porcupine and too big for a marten," was all John could offer.

*Skiing on Snake Creek*

The intruder was after something, but a thorough search of the cabin area offered no clue as to what. The large flakes of snow falling around us distorted the size and shape of the animal's tracks, so we could not even determine by this means who our nocturnal visitor was. We would just have to wait and see if it returned.

By midnight, we had finished entering the daily notes in our journal, and still our mysterious visitor had not returned. We turned in, confident that it had abandoned its quest.

*November 2nd*
Like clockwork, the clanging, rustling sounds came again. We jumped up from the table and crowded in front of the window to peer into the darkness. This time we caught a brief glimpse of a wolverine sorting through the jumbled pile of tools.

Few wild animals are as vicious and cunning as these half-wolf, half-bear creatures. They are cursed by trappers especially, for once a wolverine makes a trapline its feeding station, it is relentless in pilfering the kills not rightfully its own. Wolverines have been known to follow a trapper on his line for weeks, harassing him by stealing his axe or other tools and in the end forcing him to relocate.

They are strong beasts, with powerful jaws and sharp teeth. Many a wolverine has found its way intö a temporarily vacated cabin and wreaked havoc inside.

"Now what in the dickens could he want that's out there?" I asked.

"I don't know but we've got to convince him to leave. Get some pots, Jo."

The question of whether or not to open the door to scare him off was answered when banging the pots and shouting from inside didn't move the animal an inch. He let out a guttural, hissing snarl and then burrowed deeper in the pile of axes, saws and winter travelling gear.

"Nasty temper."

"Nasty problem, you mean! Let's try opening the door. Maybe we can scare him off that way."

We shone the lantern light into the animal's eyes and shouted. The wolverine countered by baring its fangs in a vicious sneer but made no move to depart. Next we tried the pots, with better results. The noise had reached crystal shattering levels, leaving the prowler no other choice but to beat a retreat.

When the stinging sound of metal on metal faded, we stuck our noses out into the absolute silence of the night air for one last check. There was no wolverine in sight, just its tracks heading into the woods west of the cabin.

*November 3rd*

Wolverines are not so easily diverted when you have what they want. What our fellow sought was a complete mystery to me, and when he returned for a third time to resume his search, he was not well received.

Nine o'clock was his established prowling hour, and when he failed to show, we relaxed our watch at the windows. About midnight, though, the familiar noises resumed. I was stretched out on the bed reading when I heard the ruckus outside the window.

"He's back," I announced as I peered out the window," and you won't believe this, but he's managed to tear my snowshoes off the wall and he's eating one of them."

"I'd believe anything at this point," John retorted. He removed the .303 from the wall, checked the bolt mechanism, slid a bullet into the chamber and adjusted the safety catch.

"I'll only use it if I have to but at least it's ready," he replied to my questioning look.

The pots were again hauled out but they were not the deterrent we hoped for. The wolverine took a swipe at the air and issued a malicious snarl but continued eating the webbing on my snowshoes.

"I'm not setting foot outside this door until that guy is out of commission," John proclaimed as he shut the door. This didn't sit right with me, because one of the major concerns we had discussed at length was preserving the sanctity of the wilderness environment we lived in. I understood that we couldn't allow the animal to terrorize us, but killing him seemed a desperate move.

On the other hand, our visitor had apparently lost all fear of man. If we kept using non-violent means to ward him off, would he attack without warning some evening when we left the cabin? Suddenly I recalled that I had made a trip to the privy less than twenty minutes ago. Had the wolverine been a few minutes earlier who knows what might have happened.

"The pots — one more go. If they don't work then you better kill it."

The wolverine made his first advance toward the door when I tried to scare him off with the noise. He pounced quickly, but my nerves were so taut, I just threw the pans at him and slammed the door shut.

"Okay, go to the window and stay there. I want you to tell me if I get him," John commanded.

I could see the outline of the powerful body as the lantern, set at John's feet by the open door, cast a stream of light on the snow. The wolverine was crouched over the shoe again, working the leather straps with his teeth. The bullet exploded from the gun and instantly killed the animal, thus ending his nocturnal visits. Once the carcass was dumped into the river, my peace of mind was restored.

# Blanket of White

*November 5th*

Snake Creek, the only waterway in our immediate area that is frozen over, is now a two-lane highway where we spend many hours racing back and forth on skis. What a different world it is with the blanket of white smoothing the surface for easy travel. All the twisted, brushstrewn channels we battled through on our summer trips to Big Island Lake are lost under cover — the obstacles frozen beneath the surface, to be forgotten during the seven months of the northwest's most challenging season.

We are blessed with five below temperatures and if our guesses prove correct, the thermometer will hover around this mark for a short while yet before taking the serious plunge. The air is so dry, it feels warmer than this, so dressing for long ski trips involves little more than adding a windbreaker over our cotton turtlenecks and oiled wool sweaters, and donning woolen toques and mitts (although by midday these aren't needed). Just to be safe, we each carry a day pack with down vests and dry wool socks, along with lunch, our gorp mixture (oatmeal, raisins, peanuts, carob chips and coconut), one pot for soup, matches, and our lightweight swedesaw. Noon hour campfires are needed more to dry out sweat-soaked clothing than for warmth, so that we don't get chilled on our way home. Already we can cover many more miles than we thought we were in shape for.

Animals tracks are everywhere. With foot pads and pawprints so easily identifiable in the snow, we make frequent stops to investigate the recent activities of rabbits, marten, wolverine and moose. What appears at first glance to be a silent world is in fact a playground with the local happenings recorded on a tablet for others to see.

*November 6th*

Our snow stakes record twelve inches of accumulated snowfall, much of which we have banked around the outside cabin walls to prevent loss of heat. High winds, however, have reduced the effectiveness of this mea-

*The cabin at minus forty*

sure. Our modest pre-trip research into prevailing weather patterns indicated a predominantly west to east system. But something is amiss — the cold winter winds have been blowing up the valley from east to west and charging into the clearing with a vengeance. The cabin's southeast corner takes the brunt of the gale-like force.

Most heat loss occurs when the front door is opened. Even if it's only slightly ajar, a blast of icy wind tears through the cabin. We decided to build a front porch which could also serve as extra storage space.

After breakfast we nailed a fifteen by seven foot, heavy-duty plastic tarp around the veranda roof supports. The opening is an overlapping cover at one end of the long closed-in alleyway that can be fastened tightly to keep the winds from blowing in. The only problem with the plastic walls became obvious when we went back inside and realized we couldn't enjoy the view from the front windows. We felt as though we were in a permanent snowstorm.

There was a simple solution though. We cut out two square holes in the tarp, and using our awl and wax thread, sewed in two transparent plastic bags. These are strong enough to withstand the wind and allow us to see out perfectly! The final step was to weight the end of the entire length of tarp with blocks of wood and then snow. As long as the plastic doesn't billow or flap in the wind it isn't likely to tear.

*November 8th*

Because the feeder streams no longer contribute to the river's flow, the water level between the South Nahanni's banks shrinks daily. The new and thicker layers of shore ice that have formed break off as the snow accumulates and the water supporting them drops. The grinding and bumping as these floating ice sheets are carried downriver can be heard throughout the clearing.

When we stepped outside early this morning the freeze-up was nearing its later stages. A sheet of ice, six inches thick, had set more than halfway across the river. Home shore, a shallow rocky bar, was firm enough to walk on, while a narrow open section on the opposite bank ran the remaining force of the river.

A hissing chorus, the sound of minute ice crystals attaching themselves to the edge of the shelf, was accompanied by low rumbles as pieces of ice were forced through this narrow channel. The ice slabs that manage to get through this section float downriver, where, just a quarter of a mile further, they fan out from shore to shore.

We fish where the gaps between these floating islands are the widest.

Mastering the art of fishing in half frozen, half open water takes practise. We are becoming quite proficient at predicting where the ice sheets will split as they leave the narrows — the key factor in knowing were and when to cast. We bait our large spinners with moosemeat and try to glide them over the ice shelf so they drop into one of the spaces of open water. We have to keep a watchful eye on the ever shifting ice blocks and try to stay one step ahead of the approaching flow. If a sharp edged slab of ice gets too near the spot where spinner and line are sunk, the effort of casting is for naught.

My early attempts at fishing were a disaster, but the thought of landing one of the northern monsters under such conditions spurred me on. Today proved to be my day.

I had just cast my line into a narrow but long stretch of open water when a fish grabbed the lure, and with a lunge, headed upriver.

The line played out so rapidly, even after the drag was set, that I feared I was going to follow the giant all the way to Whitehorse. It had me on the line!

If it swam along the edge of the flow for much longer I could forget about the fresh Dolly Varden fillets for dinner.

I put every bit of muscle I had into reeling my catch in. As the line zigzagged back and forth, I braced myself on the shore, reeled in as fast as I could and tugged back on the line while shouting to John to catch me if I was suddenly pitched forward.

Suddenly the flopping monster rose to the surface — not a great flying leap but a determined effort to spit out the lure nonetheless. My guess at the size of this Dolly Varden was confirmed. It looked as hefty as some of the building logs we had heaved around to use as firewood. John was beside me now, cheering me on.

"There's more than one dinner in that one Jo!" he yelled.

Caught up in the fight, I yanked at the line and reeled in more. A lurch on the line sent me staggering forward, closer to the edge of the ice shelf —the Dolly was swimming under me!

Forgetting the danger, I planted myself at the water's edge and shoved the tip of the rod down into the slush to prevent the line from rubbing against the ice.

"Reel him in," John yelled. I did, using the last reserve of energy I had.

I strained to lift the wildly flopping Dolly out of the river, my rod almost bent in half, my arms trembling. With John's help, I managed a final yank to dump the fish on the shore ice. My first great fishing expedition was over, and the result — twelve and a half pounds of trout.

*November 9th*

Perhaps it's because the snow cover helps camouflage the cabin and the clearing, or maybe simply a lucky day, but twice we were able to observe wildlife without their seeing or smelling us.

The first was a wolverine racing along the opposite shoreline. Twice, at narrow sections of open water, it hesitated, as if wanting to cross over. We got a good look at it through the field glasses — its coat of black fur, with a blonde streak along the side, was sleek and thick. Its powerful legs carried it easily through the snow. It is not a pretty animal despite the sheen of its coat. When it faced us we could see its sharp fanged teeth and the long curved claws protruding from its front paws. I was reminded of our one unwanted visitor and was greatly relieved when this wolverine continued upriver by way of the far shore.

Later in the afternoon a small band of caribou, one large male, two females and a young buck, appeared in the clearing. We watched, intrigued, at the window as the four trotted along. We thought they were probably headed for their winter feeding grounds. Their hooves clicked in unison as they moved one behind the other, taking each step on the slippery surface with utmost care. When the lead male stopped for a drink, each caribou in turn followed his example.

I decided to try out a trick a miner from Tungsten had told me. If I assumed a "bicycle position" while lying on my back, and pedalled slowly, the caribou, naturally inquisitive animals, would come up to me to investigate. I had made it as far as the picnic table before I was spotted. In a flash of movement, he jerked his head high and made a hundred-and-eighty degree turn. Like a choreographed dance number, the three trailing members spun on their heels as well, and in seconds all four were out of sight. Disappointed, I returned to the cabin.

Five minutes later, the entourage returned, more hesitant now in their move across the clearing. I remained inside this time, hoping not to spook them again.

There were no stops for idle sniffs or a drink from the river — the four moved cautiously forward. But again, the lead buck stopped abruptly, arched his antlered head and turned about. Like dominoes tripped to fall in succession, the other caribou followed his lead back to where they came from. Spooked again.

Our Canadian flag, flapping wildly in the stiff breeze was one possible reason for the caribou's flight. The other was simply our presence. The cabin area must have reeked of human smells, a terrifying unknown to these wild animals.

*November 10th*

It was a cold twenty-five degrees below when we awoke to the clamour of ice blocks roaring downriver. The reverberation of sound as the cracking and crunching echoed across the still air caused a deafening pandemonium. The noise sent us bounding out the door, not even dressed for the cold weather. When we reached the shoreline the trembling, rolling activity of the ice had subsided.

"The blocks must be jammed downriver," John guessed.

Whatever the cause, the show was not over yet. Just a hundred feet from us, a buildup of ice chunks spread across the entire width of the river. Slowly, the running water was being halted, as more and more chunks from upriver eased in. We could hardly believe that this wild river was being stilled by another natural force.

"Hear that gurgling beneath us?" I asked John. Between the gelid river bottom and the top cover of ice water was trapped, and we could hear the sound of it lapping against the ice shelf. The river was active yet!

The brief lull was shattered when a grinding crack exploded in our ears. Somewhere upriver the entrapped flow had found a weak spot in the ice and was crashing through the blockade. The river spilled over the shore ice and the mass of blocks like lava spewing out of a volcano.

We had ventured out onto the shelf, as far as we considered safe, but once the flooding began we headed quickly for more solid ground. In the nick of time. The weight of the flood water on the ice shelf had proved too much, and in one mighty crash it dropped some two feet in the middle.

This sequence of events repeated itself several times during the day. At midnight, when the sounds of an active South Nahanni had not been heard for over an hour, we took the lantern down to investigate. The river was frozen solid.


*November 12th*

Splitting wood is now a big task. Over the autumn we collected a thirty-cord supply of two types of wood — driftwood and discarded pieces of building trees. The trees split easily in the cold temperatures under our six-pound splitting axe. What moisture remains in the wood has frozen solid, so a good blow with the splitter will halve a block cleanly. The driftwood, although dry, is another story, and I have developed a theory to explain its cantankerous nature.

Trees uprooted from their banks during the peak runoff periods get caught in snyes, shallow bars, or the upper reaches of islands, and eventually dry out enough to be called driftwood. These derelict timbers once grew close to the river's edge, where they spent their entire lifetime exposed to fierce winds. They are, therefore, by nature, twisted. When trying to split these blocks, one can never hope for a clean break. Repeated chops are necessary to break down not one set of fibres but a multitude. Some of the pieces John and I split looked as though we had peeled them apart, rather than chopped them with a splitter.

The wood is dry though. It lights up in a jiffy, and we're glad to have it (once it's split) for starting fires and raising the temperature of the stove.

At times we turn the job into a contest. We remove pieces of wood from the pile, set them on end like a battalion of soldiers and then systematically move around the field halving and quartering each one. We take turns as splitter and gatherer of the split pieces. It is considered a victory if the person splitting can move around the circle in one round of blows and not have to take a second swing at any particular log. Of course, different rules are applied to driftwood.

Once the pile of splits is big enough we shuttle it inside through the trapdoor to be stacked and dried for use.

*November 18th*

For the past two months the weather has been erratic — extremely cold temperatures alternating with brief warmups. A few days ago the temperature dropped to forty below overnight, and, to make it worse, the fire died out. When we awoke the cabin was like an icebox, which started us thinking about ways to alleviate the discomfort of getting dressed on such mornings. Our strategies are different, but both work well. John has taken to wearing trousers and a shirt to bed. I leave my clothes under the pillow for the mornings when it is my turn to rise first, and I squirm into them while still in my sleeping bag.

Today we took advantage of the minus twenty-five degree temperature to dismantle the stovepipes and take them outside to scrape the creosote from their inside surfaces. Using green wood causes this carbon sediment to condense in the pipes — as much as half an inch thick. We'll have problems with stack fires it we don't clean it out, because when it dries, it flakes off, falls down the pipes and lodges in the elbows or creases. If the temperature in the stack ever gets hot enough, it will ignite these deposits.

After breakfast we let the stove die out and, while waiting for the pipes to cool off, we cleaned the woodbox with a shovel and dumped the ashes into our kybo pit. This done, we stood on the stove top, took apart the pipes, and ran them outside to be cleaned.

In ten minutes the stove was reassembled and a fire set at once, because in the short time we'd been busy the indoor thermometer had dipped below the freezing mark.

"Just wait until midwinter," said John. "We'll finish the job in two minutes!"

*November 20th*

It was late when we buttoned up the cabin to retire. The moon, just a shade from being full, cast beams of silver light through the windows. Without the lantern on, we could make out every detail of the snowy landscape beyond — the shadows of rod-straight spruce with their scraggy lower branches, the white disc glowing out of a haze of cloud atop Snow White, the mountains' lofty snow-crusted peaks etched on a midnight sky.

About four in the morning, John nudged me awake. "Jo, listen. The wolves!"

From somewhere beyond the clearing came the sonorous howls, rising in pitch and intensity by the minute.

"They're close," I shuddered, as I rolled myself into a tight ball and curled up with John's arm tight around me.

"It's okay. They're just out for a moonlight stroll." But I could feel the tenseness in his muscles and his heart thumping rapidly.

Wolves are known to hunt in larger packs during the winter months, when food is scarce, and the time of the full moon offers more light for hunting. The lament we were hearing could well be the pack moving on after they had taken an animal down. It sounded as though hundreds had gathered for a group keening session.

Even when the howls ceased, I could not relax. The pack sounded so close. I checked the clock — 4:15 — still a few hours until wake up. I buried my head in the sleeping bag and clenched my pillow for dear life.

John was already dozing again when I peeped out from under my covers. The moon was still up and I gazed out the window, concentrating on the flag as it rolled about in the wind — anything to lull me to sleep again. Suddenly I noticed something big move from behind the picnic table.

"There's an animal outside!" I cried out. I didn't realize I was watching a wolf until a second form emerged from the shadows, and a third by the flagpole. John woke when I screamed and went to the window. His curiosity was as strong as my cowardice. Angry with myself, I joined him, peering into the darkness.

We counted four wolves sauntering around the cabin and sixteen on the river, and as if their numbers weren't enough, their size was shocking. I was sure that each of the wolves we observed at close range from the window weighed well over a hundred pounds. The largest one stood about three and a half feet high. His long agile legs and powerful haunches supported a massive body. These were indeed a well fed lot.

John badly wanted a picture of one of these oversized members of the canine family. In an effort to attract them to the window, he used the flash unit of our camera as a beacon. I remained in complete control for two rounds of this, but then I became unstrung. His desire to have the wolves come within two inches of the window was, in my eyes, an invitation to trouble. Two panes of plexiglass acting as barrier between man and wolf just wasn't enough for me, and I implored him to put the thing away.

I retreated to bed and tried curling back into my covers. A scratching noise from the wall next to the bed sent me flying onto the floor.

I was trembling from head to toe. I got up and walked from window to window, slowly, because I wasn't sure my legs would support me.

John had the camera ready and was waiting by the window next to the door to see if a wolf would try getting into the porch.

"Promise me you won't go outside," I pleaded.

"Jo, it's okay. We're safe in here."

"I know we're safe inside but don't go outside."

"If you know we're safe how come you're so scared?"

"I don't feel I know enough about wolves. Neither do you! Anything could happen."

"They won't hurt us, Jo. They're more interested in what's out there. Honest. Look — over by the line, there's two of them."

The pair had taken a liking to some clothing that was frozen on our outdoor clothesline. They leapt at the cardboard stiff T-shirts and sweaters as if these objects possessed demon personalities of their own. They would back off after a swipe at the clothing and watch it swing to and fro. When the motion ceased, they would spring again. Not until one of the pair sank his teeth securely into the rigid sleeve of one sweater and brought it to the ground did they really get a chance to attack. What a battle! They literally chewed the clothes to bits while fighting over the choicest pieces between themselves.

While this was taking place, the other two wolves snooped around, chewed bits of rope and wood and generally made themselves at home.

John and I moved back and forth from bed to kitchen table, to front door and woodshed, depending where the sounds of scratching came from. For what seemed an eternity we watched and listened. I prayed that the absence of any food or garbage would convince the four that they should move on.

Twenty minutes later they wandered down to the river where the rest of the pack was assembled. I was so relieved I almost broke into tears.

*November 21st*
With the first light of dawn we were up to survey the damage done. Shreds of clothing lay scattered in the snow beneath the clothesline and fifty feet beyond, where one of the wolves had torn a handerchief to shreds. The lashings that held the stretched moosehide taut had been severed but, surprisingly, the hide itself was left untouched.

Toilet paper, yards of it, unravelled and thoroughly chewed up, covered the ground in the area of the kybo, and the fluorescent markers that had outlined the boundaries of the heliport were either missing or mangled beyond recognition. To top off the general mess, the axe — our best one — was gone. It had been left, sunk into a log, at our water hole — the very spot where the wolves had gathered.

Of the four axes we'd started out with, one was lost to the Nahanni in our first attempt at chopping a water hole in the ice, and now the wolves had the best of the remaining three. We searched frantically for that axe — carefully following each set of prints, on the lookout for some clue. They had carried if off instead of dragging it through the snow, which made our attempt at detective work futile. After a few hours we called the search off, resigning ourselves to having only two axes, a double-bitted and a splitter. Neither one was a prize implement. The loss weighed on our minds all day and repeatedly the question arose — what would a wolf do with an axe?

*November 22nd*
One of the most immediate problems of living in a one-room cabin is how to best use the space. Picture a fifteen by twenty-one-foot area serving as laundromat, workshop, bakery, and home. Organization has become even more important now that cold weather forces us to do more of our chores indoors. Strict fuel rationing means that even reading and relaxation must be limited.

Since the wolves discovered the tastiness of our laundry, we have strung indoor lines around the support posts, close to the stove. Washing is usually done on foul weather days when the outdoors is less inviting. Normally two or three trips a day are made to the waterhole, but on laundry day more than a dozen buckets of water are brought in and heated in every available pot.

To make such days even more productive we bake bread and desserts, and the floor is often littered with chips from a woodworking project. The cabin becomes a disaster area, and we make a joke of it by heaping one mess atop another.

At the end of the day we have a mass clean up, then enjoy clean clothes, good eats, and some new addition to the home. Life indoors normally falls somewhere between this chaos and impeccable neatness — almost impossible to maintain in cabin life.

No matter how inhospitable the weather, certain chores have to be done outdoors — like gathering water and chopping wood. One item we have sorely needed since the recent snowfalls is a sled. We have three cords of driftwood stacked across the river, and a sled would make transporting it much easier. After days of searching John has located two sturdy birch poles with just the right natural curve needed for sled runners. The underside of each has been levelled off with a surform plane, a flat board nailed on top of them, and lashing loops attached to the four corners. Now we have another chore to keep us busy!

*December 3rd*

When, on December 1st, we awoke to a balmy minus three degrees, the air felt like a breath of spring. The grey jays, which we had not seen for quite some time, returned to the site, all round and plump from hordes of moosemeat scraps we had left for them on the bird feeder. The marten, in his bushy winter coat, sniffed about under the picnic table, in the outdoor veranda and through the woodpile, leaving not an inch of ground untracked. Despite the grey jays dislike of the marten, it is, in our eyes, almost a household pet. When I speak some jibberish to him, he cocks his head to one side in a manner that almost persuades me he understands every word. He won my heart this morning when I looked out the kitchen window to find him perched on the sill, his button eyes searching for a way to get in.

Later in the day we were outside sawing deadfall into lengths when we discovered that the marten, along with his mate, had taken up residence in our brushpile. We had stopped to rest for a minute, on a log near the entranceway to their hideout, when the jabberings of martentalk issued from within the small chamber. It sounded like a rip-roaring good fight was in full swing. The loud chatter and squeals were, no doubt, not intended for our ears, but listening to it reinforced our feeling that these animals possess almost human traits.

*December 5th*

The warm front left us as quickly as it had come. The mercury dropped overnight and snow-laden clouds moved in.

Before too much snow fell we wanted to tour the length of Snake Creek and look for inhabited beavers' lodges.

More snow would conceal the air holes, which, in a lodge that is occupied, are faintly discoloured and therefore easily detected.

We set off in the twilight of early morning, under a sky that threatened more snow before nightfall. Had we not known where the lodges were, it would have been difficult to tell one from the snowcovered mounds of deadfall, bushes, and rocks. Everything looked like a beaver lodge that day, and it took some time before we found the one house near Three Moose Lake that showed signs of habitation. After brushing aside the top layer of snow we found a yellow crust surrounding a single air space.

We pressed our ears to the hole hoping to hear snoring beavers, but there were no sounds from the chamber. We covered the dome with handfuls of snow and made a hasty trip homeward, for the weather was much colder than when we had left home that morning.

The creek seemed void of life this afternoon, with us the only living creatures for miles. Silence, solitude and freedom from time restrictions are among the priceless qualities of a wilderness outing, but today our two-mile trek was a lonely one — until a pair of lovely winged creatures crossed our path.

Two ptarmigans waddled atop the crust of snow and disappeared behind a mound of small bushes that looked more like mushroom caps with the buildup of snow on their upper branches. These birds had snowy white plumage with just a tinge of pink, making it difficult to distinguish them from the surface they walked on. After seeing them, I felt less isolated. There was still life in the valley.

We stopped to investigate the moose sleeping areas — large patches of packed down snow, with impressions of antlers, legs, and bodies.

The rest stations were scattered, some under trees and others in open pastures. If we were to draw any conclusion about when, where and how moose sleep, it would appear that the answer is, Anytime. Anywhere. Anyhow.

*December 10th*

The days are growing shorter. From ten until two the skies are their brightest, but even then it's more twilight than daylight. The remaining hours are dark. The lantern operates fourteen hours a day, and during severe storms we are bound to it morning and night.

Our world becomes one of books when the weather turns foul. While swirls of snow and wind beat against the cabin walls, we spend hours at the kitchen table, reading or recording notes in our journal. For two days I buried myself in Leon Uris' *Trinity,* stopping only long enough to grab a bite to eat. I followed this up with *Hotel,* by Arthur Hailey, and am now

engrossed in the biography *Eleanor and Franklin.* We have our academic
books, which we read chapters of now and again, but the novels are hardly set down once we begin them — it's as close to going to the movies as
we'll get!

I've noticed John leafing through two of my textbooks, one on health
and the other on exercise physiology. I believe he's beginning to understand my feelings about daily exercise and proper nutrition — a
dedication he once considered fanatical. Likewise his accounting texts
have proved interesting reading material for me — once I figured out the
meaning of debit and credit.

We began preparations for our Yuletide season with twenty-four inches of
snow and no doubts about a white Christmas. If anything, we may be
snowed in. During a lull in the blizzard, we went in search of a suitable
spruce and found a perfectly proportioned one to set up next to the kitch-
en table. An evening spent decorating was a test of our resourcefulness.
From our first days in the valley we had been storing package wrappers
and other scraps in our box of "collectibles," for use in small projects.
Digging into it, we found tinfoil, which we cut into strips for tinsel, egg
cartons, toilet tissue rolls, magazine cutouts and wool for tree ornaments
(bells, angels, Christmas trees and Santa Claus faces), as well as popcorn
and cranberries to string into long chains. The result is a cheery, well
adorned and truly individualistic tree that symbolizes a true wilderness
Christmas — home-decorated the way trees used to be.

Our wreath is hung in the bedroom window, with a single candle lit
beneath it. We fashioned a frame with spare wire, wove the spruce boughs
around it, and arranged pine cones throughout. The finishing touch is a
red bandanna tied in a bow in the centre.

I've already begun my Christmas baking and am sparing no excess.
Cakes, cookies, muffins, sweetbreads, candies and squares — the cabin
smells of delicious sweetness.

*December 20th*
Thanks to the local pilots we have something of a neighbourhood reputa-
tion. "The crazy greenhorns wintering in the valley," is one we've heard,
but similar versions, we are told, are bandied about as far away as Fort
Liard. Apparently a nurse there doubts that we'll ever come out alive.
Hearing this only convinces us that a modern day "moccasin telegraph"
exists in the north.

The growing knowledge of our presence means occasional visits even in
winter. Today the warm western winds were blowing into the valley, rais-

*John reading at kitchen table*

ing the temperature well above minus forty degrees — a good day for flying.

Dwight, a miner from Tungsten, took advantage of the weather break
to fly the forty air miles from his camp to visit.

He and his companion, Lloyd, were flying a Cessna — a model old-
timer that has seen thousands of miles of mountains and rough terrain in
its airborne lifetime. The antique requires special care though, and
Dwight wrapped a blanket over the engine before he joined us for coffee.

Throughout our hour-long visit he kept a watchful eye on the sky and
the thermometer. The air was cooling off rapidly.

Dwight is a young and adventuresome man who tells stories with a
twinkle of mischief in his eyes. As he spoke of his flying experiences we began to warm up to him, realizing that he shared our passion for the adventure of mountainous country. Unlike many of the men who live in the
dorm at Tungsten and spend most of their free time in camp, Dwight has
a small cabin and trapline that he visits every chance he gets. On holidays
he flys into the mountains to hunt for dall sheep or mountain goats, landing his Cessna on an alpine meadow and then walking for miles along the
precipitous ridges of the Ragged Range with a pack of provisions on his
back.

When he just feels like getting away, he'll land his plane (on wheels)
on gravel bars along a river and spend an afternoon fishing. He listened
enthusiastically to our own wolverine, wolf and moose stories. In truth,
he was ready to wring our necks when he heard of our dumping the
wolverine into the river that night.

"Next time anything like that happens, skin the thing and you'll fetch a
good price for it at the auction."

He can't be more than twenty-five, but with seven years' experience in
the mine, a trapline, his plane, another house in British Columbia that he
built himself, and the headful of memories from good times on backwoods
trails, he's a rich man who has already lived several lifetimes. His modesty
and self-sufficiency make him a thoroughly admirable fellow to our way
of thinking.

A look at the sky ended our table talk. Dark clouds were moving in and
the thermometer had dropped twelve degrees. It was time to warm up the
Cessna and get Lloyd to work for the afternoon shift.

The plane would not start. Dwight leaned on the propeller and put all
his muscle into whipping it to turn over the engine, but on each
downward thrust, the blade spun, slowed, and then stopped. The engine
had to be warmed up — and quickly. For a frantic twenty minutes we
split pieces of dry wood, carried down a tarp that would act as a shield

against the wind, and set a fire beneath the plane's engine. With the barrier up, the heat was contained and the engine soon thawed. John and I were fearful that oil dripping from the engine might catch fire, but Dwight seemed so in control of the situation that we held our tongues. Given what we had heard over coffee, he knew better than us. He gave the propeller another try. It turned over immediately.

"That box we brought in," Dwight yelled over the whirl of the blades. "There's Christmas oranges and doughnuts for you! I'll try and get in with a turkey if the weather holds!" With that, he smiled and climbed aboard.

*December 24th*
Christmas Eve...It is a cold clear night in the valley.

The cabin was especially cheerful with our stockings hung near the tree and candles burning in every window. After dinner we decided to go snowshoeing. A special eggnog, made from powdered eggs and milk and spiced with cinnamon was brewing for our return.

The squeak and crunch of our snowshoes echoed in the night air as we stepped through the soft powder snow that covered the hard packed surface of ice crystals beneath. We walked up and down the river, singing carols as we went. The sky was ink black, with a patchwork of high cloud cover, but the moon and stars shone bright enough to light our way.

The cold stung our noses and cheeks and nipped at our fingers, but the peaceful world we walked through seemed like Bethlehem itself.

We serenaded the trees, the sky and the animals we couldn't see, until our voices grew hoarse and our faces numb from the exposure. Our Christman Eve celebration has made me even more appreciative of the quiet and pure world we live in. An aura of serenity and unmasked solitude surrounds us daily, but at times like this, when our surroundings are overpowering in their loveliness and the silence of the night is so absolute it rings in my ears, I find myself floating over the surface of the snow, enveloped by a warm contented glow.

*December 25th*
"Jo, it's only seven o'clock," John mumbled.

"Time to get up," I ordered as I leapt onto the freezing cold floor and skipped around the cabin, gathering pieces of kindling and firewood to fill the woodbox of the stove.

I stole a side glance at the kitchen table. John had secretly filled our stockings during the night. They were brimming and bulging with what was unmistakably fruit. Where had he gotten it, and how had he managed to hide it?

The coffee pot gurgled and pancakes and bacon were soon sizzling in the frying pans. A day of favourite foods was in store for us — bits of this and that we had saved for this very occasion.

"Too early do you think to phone in the weather?"

"The Sandes will be up," I answered.

John flipped the radio on and gave it a few minutes to warm up before calling B.C. Yukon Air Services. A gruff voice was giving a weather report from a location a couple of hundred miles south of us. When the call was over John tried to make contact.

"86 Watson — This is XNL 999...Over"

"999 — This is 86 Watson. Go ahead."

"Merry Christmas, Mrs. Sande! How do you read us this morning?"

"About 3 by 5 with some static."

John handed me the small microphone so I could give my Merry Christmas as well.

"Merry Christmas to you, Joanne. How's the weather up there this morning?"

"Its not a bad day here in the valley. Temperature is minus thirty degrees. Sky is broken to the blue. Ceiling at about six thousand feet. Darker clouds moving in from the west. Over."

"We're down in low cloud here. Might get some snow today."

"Well, we hope your Christmas is a happy family reunion. I suppose all the kids will be up to the house for dinner?"

"Yes, it should be a full house. You two have a nice day, too."

"Thank you. It will be a quiet one but we're looking forward to talking with our families later on. Good day now. 999 clear."

"86 Clear."

John turned the dial to our long distance frequency that connected us with the Canadian National Telecommunications operator in Whitehorse, Yukon. We had two crystals in our radio; one that gave us local contact and the second, operator assisted long distance calls. We'd have our ears cocked to listen for SR-1652 (our second call sign) while opening our gifts and preparing dinner.

One large box sat underneath the tree. It was a gift from the Moores, given to us the day we'd left Ontario back in May. It had travelled across Canada with us, the wrapping still intact despite half a dozen weak moments during our first seven months when one or the other of us threatened to open it before its time. Now, after months of jiggling it and guessing at its contents, we unwrapped it with great ceremony.

"I've got an idea," John said. "Let's take turns removing one present at a time. This thing's loaded!"

John went first.

He closed his eyes, stuck his hand into the box and felt around.

"Okay, this is it!" he announced and like a magician pulling a rabbit out of a top hat, he produced a large chocolate bar — pure gold.

For two hours this went on, until the table top was covered with delicacies. After seven months of simple fare the compulsion to drop to my knees at the sight of smoked oysters, paella, chocolates, cheeses, imported coffee, and tea was overwhelming. Besides food there were hand creams, perfume, aftershave, Christmas decorations, pocketbooks, two more cassette tapes, a puzzle for John and a needlepoint kit for me.

The remainder of the day we spent making fresh bread, reading, and listening for our call sign. Around five o'clock a faint and garbled SR-1652 came over the radio.

"This is SR-1652, Go ahead, operator."

"I have a caller from Ontario on the line.

"Go ahead, radio"

"Merry Christmas!" I yelled into the microphone. "Can you hear me?"

"Loud and clear, Joey," Dad laughed. "Is John listening, too, or is he off tracking down another moose?"

"I'm right here, Jim. Boy, it sure is good to hear your voice. How's everything at home?"

Mother, grandmother and brothers were waiting on the line to speak with us — breathless as we were and trying to cram as much in two or three minutes as they could. Their voices came over the speaker crisply, a "5 by 5", or perfect reception, filling the cabin's every corner. Our radio did not have an earpiece, so we could hear everything being said without having to take turns listening.

Finally Peter, second youngest in the family, got on the line.

"Merry Christmas, Jo. Over. Merry Christmas John. Over. How are the woolies from the North doing? Over. Things are great here. Over. I'm looking for a car to buy. Over. He hadn't as much as taken a breath in between!

John and I were so caught off guard we didn't try to interject. The tears of laughter were streaming down our cheeks. He had obviously been briefed on radio protocol.

*Nahanni Christmas*

"Did you two get all that?" Dad chuckled.

"We did."

The reception worsened, making it necessary for us to rush our final comments.

"We're fine, Jim. Letters on the way [through Dwight]. We love the North! Have a Merry Christmas." John closed off before our voices faded altogether.

"SR-1652 this is the operator. Are you clear?"

"Yes, operator. Thank you. That was a good call. 1652 clear."

We were thankful we had been able to speak for so long. Often it didn't work out so nicely. A call can be cut off abruptly, or sometimes one party gets good reception and the other not a thing. We turned to dinner preparation, overjoyed at having shared our Christmas greetings with family.

To produce a dinner of the finest cuisine and create an atmosphere comparable to the most exclusive of dining rooms required a fair amount of imagination under the circumstances, but we had devoted several evenings to preparing for it. The table was set elegantly, candles were lit, and our best clothing donned. John had gone to great pains to produce the most intricate of napkin arrangements, and these were tastefully placed at the top corner of each setting. The final touch was a menu card for each person, from which we could order our various courses.

Many hours had been spent producing these menu cards. Neither of us had a mastery of French so we tried a combined effort. The names would make a Frenchman shudder, but for us they possessed a unique quality all their own.

## Chez Nahanni
### Célébration de Noel

Jambon avec la Sauce Spécial

| Pommes de Terre | Légume | Asperges Pointes |
| Spuds Finnigan | Verité | de Fantaisie |

Christmas Puddance
avec la Sauce de Chef
Petit Pain de Harlow

| Café mouture | | Thé mélange |
| extraordinaire | | d'Orient |

Des cellars de Nahanni Courviseur
Vin Rouge — de la Muskeg

*January 1st*

December went out like a polar bear, producing the coldest weather
we have had to date. December 28th was a bitterly cold minus forty
degrees. The twenty-ninth saw a frigid minus forty-five and the last
two days of the month brought minus forty-eight degrees.

Our bodies have adjusted enough to the cold that we are able to continue working outdoors and even continue our long snowshoe hikes. The
only change in our routine is the length of time it takes to dress. The daily
bundle-up is quite an involved procedure.

I read once that at minus fifty degrees you're either warm or dead. At
minus fifty the body must operate at full steam ahead to maintain the
normal internal body temperature of approximately thirty-seven degrees
Celsius. Proper clothing to contain the heat is essential, as is the manu-
facturing of heat through muscular activity.

Our outdoor clothing is rated for minus sixty degrees Fahrenheit, and
when we keep on the move it's as reliable as promised. Undergarments
are equally important.

Our first layer is full length underwear of fishnet, a fabric that creates a
dead air space between skin and clothing so body moisture has a chance to
evaporate. Over this, we wear cotton turtle necks and wool shirts and
finally winter parkas and pants, each stuffed with two generous layers of
down.

We tried several combinations of footwear before deciding that two
pairs of heavy wool Wigwam Sox inside our felt lined Bush Pac boots was
ample protection and the most comfortable arrangement. On our hands,
wool mitten linings inside the Mount Everest down mitts (elbow length
mitts with large pieces of lamb's hair sewn on the back) are excellent for
working and skiing in, and roomy enough, should a hand warmer be
needed. Before donning heavy wool toques, we put on neck warmers, an
ingenious slip on collar that acts like a scarf but never comes loose or gets
in the way. Finally, the toques, a must even with hooded parkas.

We look like Pillsbury Doughboys in our full outfits, but we are free to
go anywhere, or do anything, without fear of freezing. And our suits are
lightweight and loose fitting to allow plenty of freedom of movement for
splitting wood and for general manoeuverability.

Another danger in extremely cold temperatures is that of the body
overheating. It's hard to imagine someone sweating at minus fifty, but
when heat is properly contained, it happens easily enough and once clothing becomes wet, it loses its insulating qualitites. Up to forty per cent of
body heat can be lost when no toque is worn, so removing your headgear
can release a substantial amount of excess heat. John looked like an over-

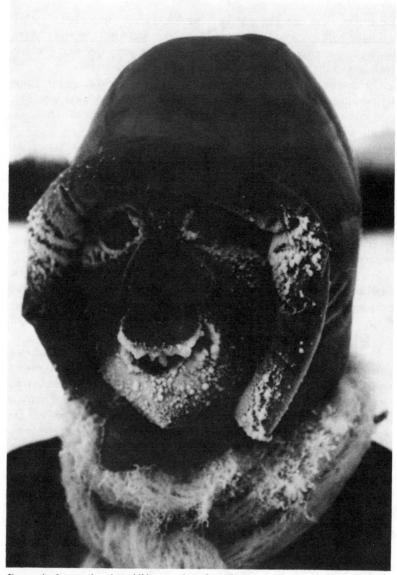

*Joanne in face mask, winter hiking at minus forty-five*

worked locomotive blowing off steam when he did this one morning during a mountain hike, but after a few minutes his body temperature dropped and he was comfortable once again.

Our down pants have full-length zippers running from thigh to ankle. By opening a small vent near the top of the pant leg, we can release the unwanted heat slowly and steadily while still on the move.

The body also needs extra fuel at cold temperatures. We eat more carbohydrates and fats (granola, peanut butter, bread fried in lard, thick soups) to get the extra calories, and on long hikes we munch regularly on snacks (squares of chocolate or gorp mixture) along with plenty of liquids, such as orange juice or sweetened tea.

Fatigue is one of the major hazards of the outdoors in sub-zero temperatures. It reduces the body's ability to continue producing heat through muscular activity. You can become sluggish, even depressed or irritable. Your skin temperature drops, fingers and toes can become frostbitten, and eventually the will to continue on is lost altogether.

On long runs or hikes we munch regularly on snacks when we stop for rests and keep an eye on each other for telltale signs of fatigue or marked heat loss. Lastly, and most important, we have come to know our limits.

### January 4th

When we rounded the bend in the river, just above the hotsprings, we could see that they were still at work despite the minus forty-eight degree temperature. While the spruce limbs on the shoreline bent under the weight of accumulated snow, the landscape at the springs was a wintry wonderland. Frost and icicles covered every bough, every twig and branch.

As we approached, we saw patches of wet, rich soil, free of snow, and vapour rising from the ground that was warmed by the underground springs. Then the long stretch of sandy beach and open water — an oasis in a winter desert.

Inland, where the source of the spring was located, the water bubbled at forty degrees, the same temperature we had recorded in the fall. Here the markings in the sand revealed mass gatherings of moose, caribou, marten, wolverine and even lynx. Surely they don't all congregate at once. We wondered how they regulated their watering times.

The extreme cold did not affect our camera, but the standing around for picture taking had to be kept to a minimum. Even with down face masks on and not an inch of flesh exposed, it wasn't long before a fire was needed to revive frozen fingers and toes.

As enchanting a place as the springs were, we could not remain in the cold very long. Following lunch and a final tour of the forests surrounding the spring, we began our trek home.

Our down masks have two slits for eye openings and another for our noses, not an article of clothing that would interest the fashion conscience outdoorsman but one that saved us from frost bitten cheeks on this day. Even a light breeze at this temperature can be devastatingly severe.

By the time we were in sight of the cabin and the reassuring signal of smoke wafting from the chimney, we were exhausted from fighting the wind and cold temperatures. Our faces were like clowns' — eyelashes coated with frost and nose and cheeks rosy red. And this was with face masks on! Without them we would not have made it ten feet beyond the cabin door.

*January 9th*

The cold snap has made trips to the waterhole a major excursion. We have to chop down, through the ice — as much as four feet in spots — before breaking through and by the time the last pail is filled, the surface of the first is covered with a thin coat of ice. Waiting for the layer to form on all the buckets reduces the volume of water lost through spillage. Water is now, more than ever, a precious commodity.

Only at bedtime is it consumed in large quantities. John read that trappers down four or five glasses of water in rapid succession before turning in for the night. Like clockwork, the person rises in the middle of the night to relieve his bursting bladder and at the same time tends to a dwindling fire box. Whereas even the mightiest of alarm clocks can go unheeded, this method guarantees a nocturnal rising.

Inside the cabin during our waking hours, it matters little what the outside thermometer reads. Only the frosted flakes on the windows, the rime on the door seams, nailheads, and latch, and the waves of cold air that roll across the floor like tumbleweed when the door is opened, indicate the frigid weather outside. The cabin remains snug. Our stove works overtime to maintain a comfortable temperature, and only when we notice how quickly the stores of wood are depleting do we give the cold a passing thought.

The cabin dweller develops a feel for his stove much as a driver does for his automobile. We have mastered the technique of how best to set it at night for various temperatures. We know how often it requires filling, what combinations of wood are best suited for the individual tasks it performs, and lastly, when and how much to open the vents for use in cooking and baking.

The claims made in the firm's advertising brochure are a chuckle. "It will easily hold a fire overnight," might well be true for temperatures above minus thirty but I fear for the person who does not tend to his firebox halfway through the night when the mercury drops below that. Another feature claimed for our stove is the "fast boil" and "slow simmer" elements, which I have yet to discover. After experimenting with several types of wood and a variety of settings on the stove's front dials, which control the amount of ventilation, I still cannot bring one surface of the stove to fast boil without having fast boil on the other. What is worse, whenever we try for a fast boil we almost suffocate in the sweltering heat.

In spite of this, our central heater is still our pride and joy. John has never once said he regrets lugging the giant onto the shores of the Nahanni, and to my way of thinking this alone proves the stove's worth!

*January 21st*
For the past week the sun has shone on the highest mountain ridges for perhaps half an hour a day. It is three months since we stood surrounded by sparkling snow crystals reflecting the light of the warm rays, and it was a welcome sight to see the first bright yellow patches on the mountain crowns to the north. Daily, the sunlight creeps further down the mountains, but we are too restless to wait for it to reach our clearing and today decided to try to get up to it.

We set off in late morning, our day packs filled with lunch, camera equipment, and our most useful accessory — sunglasses.

Our ascent up the mountain we call Pine Tree was a zig-zag pattern, so we could avoid a direct vertical climb and the formidable cliffs with their gravity defying overhangs. The moose trails proved to be the best route. In deep snow they sink up to their massive rumps, smoothing out a considerable thoroughfare. It has been said that in very high drifts moose will walk with legs bent at the knee to distribute their weight more evenly. Whatever their strategy, they're like bulldozers.

We could see the sun shining up ahead, and we raced to it in a fit of enthusiasm. When our utopia seemed but a few seconds away, we found our path blocked by a deep fissure and we were unable to climb further. The meltwater from a bowl of snow at the top of the mountain and the runoff from numerous streams that converged with this main artery had carved a gorge fifty feet deep and fifty feet wide into the side of the mountain.

"If we slide down the gorge and climb up the other side we can get to that meadow." John pointed to a small flat spot several metres above where we stood.

Just as we made our move to slide down the slope, the sun disappeared behind the Three Bears. The quest for the golden rays would have to wait for another day!

*January 22nd*

The sound of a chopper caught us completely by surprise — and smack in the middle of a colossal baking spree. Mincemeat tarts, loaves of fresh bread, and cinnamon rolls hot from the oven awaited our visitors — Pat, Lindsay, and Bruce, pilot-base-manager of Okanogan Helicopters. They emerged from the helicopter burdened with parcels, like modern day Magi.

We had first met these men in the fall. They worked for Water Survey of Canada, a branch of the federal government located in Fort Simpson. Their job was to monitor the flow of the Mackenzie River and its major tributaries year round, and this visit was in the course of a field excursion. Their visits were spaced anywhere from five to eight weeks apart but in our circumstances this was considered regular contact. Their offer to deliver our mail when they were in the vicinity was more than just an act of kindness — it was an unexpected luxury.

Over coffee and a snack we told the men about the wolves prowling around the cabin. This still troubled us.

"If they come again, do you think they'd react to a warning shot — say we fired off a couple of bullets into the air?" John asked.

"Hard to say," offered Pat. "You might be better off leaving well enough alone." Bruce nodded agreement.

"Have you ever heard of wolves doing things like that?" John asked.

No one answered. It seems the activities of our neighbourhood pack were something of a novelty.

"Just don't leave any food or garbage around." Bruce cautioned.

The mail had been forgotten in the conversation. Glancing at the heap of boxes and envelopes the men had brought, I thanked Pat for storing it all in his office at Fort Simpson.

"The parcels are no problem," he assured us. "But I've been receiving calls wondering how you're making out and I can't give very up-to-date reports when a couple of months go by and we don't see you. I guess some people have been trying to contact you by radio for weeks and can't get through. They're starting to worry that you're hurt or in trouble. I just tell them that if they're really worried they can hire Search and Rescue — at an exorbitant cost."

I hoped the question of our safety never came to that. "One thing we have to stop doing is telling all in letters. The wolf and wolverine stories should wait until the slideshows."

The men looked surprised that we would burden our relatives with scarey stories. John and I hadn't given much thought to the consequences of graphically describing events. From now on, letters would have to be toned down.

"Time to shove off," Pat announced.

Goodbyes always came to soon. We were just beginning to get warmed up — having recovered from the "tied tongue syndrome," our name for the initial period of a visit when we found ourselves fumbling around to get it all together.

Before we knew it, our guests were gone.

Alone again, the first step was to organize our mail into neat piles according to postmark dates. Some letters dated back to early November, others were more recent, and we liked to go through the assortment in order. We read letters aloud to each other, scanned the magazines and newspapers, and kept marvelling at this article or that present into the early hours of the morning — and that was only a first reading! It was four o'clock before we went to bed.

*January 27th*

Today marked the return of the moose. The great beasts have lost some of their majesty, because they no longer carry their enormous racks, but we think their return is the first sign of warmer temperatures. During the extremely cold weather, the air is as much as twenty degrees warmer in the mountains. The moose climb to these higher elevations and we saw no sign of them during December and January. Now, they are back to stay, we hope.

# Return of the Sun

On the evening of January 31st, a light sprinkling of snow tumbled out of the heavens. During the night the winds picked up, and this morning the frozen trees were creaking under the force of a howling gale. A pattern of frosty flakes covered each window. We looked outside to see snowdrifts swirling and twisting like tornadoes, sending up a fine hard snow that sounded like a spray of sand against the plexiglass. February was in with a blast of trumpets!

*February 3rd*

For three days the wind storm continued, with gusts rising to forty miles an hour — or so we estimated using our field guide book to judge the force of the wind from telltale signs. The tree tops swayed violently, the flag was nearly torn from its lanyard, and the early winter snows, which had nestled in neat mounds on the spruce boughs, were blown to the ground. These winds did not bring with them a great deal of new snow, but the old snow was swept up in billows and carried afar.

The rabbits, grey jays and marten who visited the site daily were nowhere to be seen. They, like John and me, had snuggled into their burrows to wait out the storm.

The sweeping, driving snow was fascinating to watch. It continually transformed the landscape outside the cabin windows. The river, no longer a monotonous strip of snow, wore ridges, like alluvion, of various sizes and shapes. Drifts were piled as high as two feet, like waves on a turbulent frozen sea.

Closer to the cabin, the winds had eaten away at the snowbanks to form masterful artistic strokes along the whitewashed surface. One four-foot drift extended around the front of the cabin in a cresent shape, with either end ground down to a finely tapered edge. Behind the cabin were peaked monuments and truly beautiful snow sculptures, carved by the wind.

*February 4th*

I awoke to a strange silence. A glance out the bedroom window confirmed that dawn had brought with it an air of absolute stillness. Not a twig stirred. Just as the roar of the wind and the movements of the trees had kept me awake for three nights, I was now unable to sleep in such hushed surroundings.

"Coffee is ready," I told John when he rolled out from under the covers and peered out the window.

"It's so quiet," he said. "Should be some interesting sights to photograph in the aftermath of that storm. Let's head out after breakfast."

We walked through the silent woods expecting to see uprooted timber and a mess of debris strewn about where branches had been shorn from the tree trunks. But if such damage had occurred, it was well concealed. The only evidence of the storm was the angle at which the more spindly growth was bent over. Otherwise, the setting we walked through was like a winter carnival playground. Tree stumps and alder shrubs were sculptures of windblown snow with an endless variety of gentle indentations and great sloping contours — all subject to individual interpretation.

We felt as though we were touring a museum of modern art. "Almost makes you want to take one home," John said, when we agreed that one mound resembled a beaver gnawing at the base of an alder.

On the return trip we headed off the main trails to get an update on our local inhabitants' wanderings. Only the most recent tracks would be left on the white slate.

"Over there!" John exclaimed, pointing to a patch of darkly stained snow. It was the scene of a death. Blood stains, entrails and tufts of grey white fur told the story of the final minutes of a snowshoe hare. The winds had almost completely obliterated signs of the predator.

"Could have been a bird, or maybe a lynx," I said. John spotted some markings in the snow. It had been an airborne hunter and most likely a member of the owl family.

Just a mile downriver, we had seen our first signs of the lynx — rounded pad prints with no claw marks showing and a slight smudge where the long hairs on the lynx's feet had brushed the powdery snow. All the way home we looked for the creature but without luck.

*February 7th*
Today was special indeed. For a precious five minutes the sun shone on Big Island Lake, and we were there to meet it. We had timed our arrival to the minute in order to glory in the reappearance of the one element in our lives we sorely missed.

"Here she comes," John shouted as the glaring disc peeped from behind a ridge on the Three Bears.

As the yellow light moved like a long shadow towards us, we stood breathlessly still. What a moment it was when the warmth and brightness of the rays poured down on us. Each day now it would climb higher still, above the snow sheathed rim, until it reached the cabin.

*February 8th*

The days are wonderfully peaceful, and brighter now that the sun illuminates the mountain tops in honey-coloured light, slightly warmer too. As each one passes so naturally we become more aware of our deep love for the valley and our wilderness existence.

"I could live this life for another full year and never tire of the tranquility," I said over dinner.

"And still not see everything we want to either," John responded.

Separately, when we took to the trails on snowshoes and busied ourselves with our own thoughts, and together, at night, when we shared our impressions of a day, the same feelings emerged. For weeks now we have talked about staying on.

"Would you change the cabin at all?" John asked.

"I'd add a fireplace and a separate bedroom extension, and we could go out for a few months to earn enough money for food and supplies — then come back in August and build until the snow comes."

"We could improve a few things too. Maybe rechink the walls and strengthen the woodshed roof."

"What about a dog team for winter travel?"

"Possible. But it would take a lot of time to train them. It sure would add a new dimension to life here. We could build dog houses, fence off an area beside one end of the cabin." And almost as an afterthought he added, "Hey, what about a trapline!"

These thoughts of remaining in the valley for another four seasons are fanciful, because our plans are already made. John has to return to Kingston to resume teaching in September.

Drawing up plans for a permanent log home diverts our attention from our inevitable departure from the Nahanni. The question of where we intend to settle is still up in the air but that doesn't stop the blueprinting of floor plans for another dream. For hours at night we sketch our ideas, compare notes on layouts, discuss the cost of building such a home, and talk about living in the countryside.

*February 12th*

With all the talk of what to include in our future "model home," the urge to improve upon and add to the cabin followed quite naturally.

Creosote had been seeping from the joints in the stovepipe at night, leaving drops on the stove's surfaces in the morning. When the firebox was ignited, a horrible stench of fried creosote permeated the cabin's every nook and cranny. The solution — a "creosote drip preventer" — is simply a piece of wood cut to fit around the upright section of the stack and hung from a hook off one of the sloping pipes. A small piece of flattened tin keeps the wood away from the surface of the hot pipes, and thus the problem is solved.

Our pièce de résistance is a loft bedroom. Until this alteration, the rafters, both on the east and west cabin walls, were used for storing food and supplies. As we began our eighth month in the valley, we realized that the food and toiletries in our once well-stocked larder were dwindling fast. It was now possible to use the coldest spot in the house (under the bed) for cold storage and that rafter space above the kitchen as a shelf for the less perishable items. This reorganization left the entire rafter space above our bed clear. The decision to cut out a small window in the gabled west wall and redo the loft as a bedroom was unanimous.

We took advantage of a raw February Saturday to alter the cabin's living arrangements. First, a one-foot-square opening was cut out in the gable end and a framed window was nailed in place. All that remained was to lay a floor on the loft and nail a balcony railing across two upright supports. A bookshelf, and pegs to hold the ladder in place, completed the second bedroom. There is no warmer spot on cold weather nights.

*February 14th*

I have become increasingly aware of the need for long silences when we are snowshoeing. Too much chattering back and forth disturbs the rhythm of my stride, dulls my awareness of the sights and sounds around me and shatters the inner restfulness I feel when moving forward across vast distances of the snowcovered land. In wide open spaces such as the river highway, where there are fewer points of reference to distract the eye, I can maintain this tranquility for hours.

It is not unusual for us to spend a whole morning on the move without talking. We save conversation for lunch stopovers, when we warm ourselves next to an open fire.

When our days are filled with chores, and we haven't time to ponder new thoughts and impressions, the evening hours are set aside for that purpose. A favourite activity on cold clear nights is to sit out on the cabin roof, trying to see into the darkness and listening to the muffled sounds coming from the forest.

When the moon is full, the silver light reflecting off the snow throws

*Moon rising above Snow White*

long shadows across the clearing. The northern lights dance across the inky black sky surrounding us in arms of soaring light. Always on the coldest of clear nights, when our breath crystallizes on contact with the cold dry air, there are the twinkling stars, larger than those back home in the south, or so it seems.

Sometimes a ring of light circles the moon. It has an eerie effect, like car headlights approaching you on a lone country road when the night air is saturated with fog. Perhaps this phenomenon is caused by the frosty air. One evening the ring of milky light extended far across the horizon, covering a quarter of the sky. The solitary lament of a lone wolf or the piercing screech of an owl would have suited such an atmosphere.

*February 15th*

It was dusk — that time of day when we wrap up the last of the day's chores. I was occupied with journal writing while John sorted through the first aid supplies in search of a bandaid (he had been overzealous when cutting up the fresh bread for dinner).

I am quite used to being interrupted in my work. Whenever a grey jay flutters from the nearby spruce boughs to alight on the feeder, I always, almost subconsciously, turn to watch. The rabbits too are a distraction for dusk is their play time.

A movement outside caught my attention instantly. Whatever it was striding down the path, it was big and it was black.

"John!" I called out without taking a second glance or even thinking about what I was saying. "There's a black bear next to the window!" I was frozen to the chair, and until John was beside me, I didn't make a move or a sound.

"It's no bear, " he answered, but before he finished I realized it was a wolf.

"Look, there's two more, another black and a silver." Both animals were facing the window, looking at us with steady gaze. They stood firm, peering in at the strange inhabitants. A fourth, rather scraggly member of the pack, emerged from behind a thick spruce.

The largest of the four, the black wolf who had first caught my attention, sauntered up and down the path between kybo and bird feeder like a monarch touring his domain. If he was fearful of the man scent, it was certainly not evident from his deliberate canter or steadfast gaze. He was no more than six feet from the window and as comfortable and unafraid as if he were touring his own den.

"He's huge," I gasped. "What's he up to now?"

"Just checking things out, I guess."

As darkness fell upon the clearing, John remained at the window while I went about my "wolves in the area" tactics. I fastened the door bolt, stood the ladder leading to the loft bedroom upright, and removed the gun from the wall rack. There were six bullets in the clip. I added four more, adjusted the safety, and set the weapon within easy reach. There was nothing else to do but wait and watch.

"Hear that?" John whispered.

We sprang to the bedroom window and squinted out into the blackness to catch sight of a wolf digging into the snow banked around the cabin walls. His claws scratched against the walls, John flashed the light through the window and the startled animal retreated, but soon we heard him scraping around the back shed area.

"The moose hide is on the shed roof, Jo. I wonder if they'll try to get it?"

"Get the gun, just in case," I answered. "That roof would hardly withstand the weight of four wolves."

For an hour we endured the ordeal of not knowing what the wolves were up to. Just when it seemed they had gone, we would hear more noises.

Then came a noise that snapped every nerve in my body — a ruckus at the trapdoor in the woodshed wall. From the thud and scratching it sounded as if one of the wolves was clawing at the corners of the door trying to get in. John, his face a ghastly white, screamed at me to get into the loft and take the gun.

"He's pulling the rope!" I shouted. From where I cringed I could see the coil on the cabin floor unravelling. Just days before, we had dismantled the trapdoor's pulley system so we could use the line of rope to drop the door of a rabbit trap. The rope still fed through the hole in the woodshed wall, but a length of it ran along the ground outside.

Our shouting frightened the animal enough that he let go for a moment. John regained his composure and grabbed the coil of rope at his feet, yanking it while he braced one foot against the wall. The wolf rose to the challenge, and a tug-of-war began.

Which of the wolves John battled with we do not know, but it was a powerful opponent. John's gain was shortlived. One strong yank from the other end of the rope and he was pressed against the wall, hanging on for dear life.

Whether the wolf relaxed his grip or simply chewed through the rope we don't know, but John seized the opportunity to rapidly haul the rope in, thus ending the unequal contest.

The initial shock followed by the strenuous battle had left John visibly shaken. His face was pale and drawn but there was a hint of excitement in his eyes.

"Come and sit down," I urged. "The fight is over." The absurd contest had tapped some perverse sense of humour in me and I wanted to tell John we looked like two of the three little pigs. But I didn't dare.

*February 16th*

The minute we got up, we surveyed the cabin area. Claw marks on the walls, evidence of chewing, entangled rope and mangled scraps told last night's story. And at the cache, the pack had given the area more than a cursory glance. The frozen moosemeat, stored in old gas drums on the platform, had been tantalizing but inaccessible, and as if to voice their displeasure with this, the wolves had urinated around the supports.

"I think they lost the axe they stole in November," John said incredulously.

"Why do you say that?" I began, "No, you don't mean. . ."

"Yep!" John said. "They've taken the saw."

I moaned in disbelief.

Later, we uncovered the crosscut saw along our path to Snake Creek. The thief, it appeared from the markings on the snow, was unable to carry his booty away. It had been dragged half a mile then dumped in a snow-drift.

*February 17th*

At twenty past nine in the morning, shafts of sunlight streamed in through the cabin windows. We ran outside, only half dressed, squinting our eyes and shielding our faces against the glare of the bright light glistening off the snow. For ten glorious minutes we basked in the warmth and glow of the sun's radiance. What a wonderful feeling it was!

The four months of semi-twilight and darkness that had engulfed us were over. We threw our arms around each other, laughing and shouting, tossing our mitts in the air and screaming out, "The sun, the sun — it's back, it's back!"

# Warmer Days

*February 24th*
Since our talk with Pat we've tried to make contact with home, but the airways still aren't cooperating. After dinner we turned on the radio, intending to ask the Canadian National Telecommunications operator to reassure our parents if poor reception prevented their reaching us.

The minute the operator heard our call sign she passed on a week-old message. "A woman from Edmonton has been trying to contact you."

There was a number along with the message, and a name that neither of us recognized.

"How are you reading us operator?"

"About 2 by 5 radio."

This was poor, but we asked that she put the call through to Edmonton anyway. While the phone rang at the other end, we sat wondering who we were calling.

"Go ahead radio," the faint voice said. "Your caller is on the line."

"Hello! This is Joanne." I yelled into the hand microphone. The crackle of static was so loud I could barely pick up the reply.

"...Dorcas...visit...couple weeks...March."

"Please repeat. I can't hear you."

"Dorcas Kennedy ...visit...is...okay?"

"I do not read you well. Are you coming for a visit?"

"Yes. Richard and...March."

"Reception is poor. We will call back."

"Okay."

And the line went dead.

"Looks as though we're going to have visitors for a couple of weeks," I finally said.

"Didn't Doug mention something about this in a letter?"

"Yep! He also asked us in his Christmas letter what we thought about visitors coming."

"I feel funny about this, Jo! I don't even know these people."

"Well, I've never met Richard but Dorcas lived across the street from

160

me in my final year at Queen's. You remember hearing about her coming
up north to nurse near Great Slave Lake?"

"What's she like?"

"A ball of fire. Unless she's slowed down over the last three years she's
got more energy to burn than you and me put together."

"I think you and I need time to prepare for having company around.
Do you ever wonder whether maybe the isolation has affected us in a sort
of...er...funny way?"

"You mean are we going crazy? Well, I don't know about that but
we're sure different from before we came up here."

Before we turned in we agreed that a second call was needed to finalize
plans. Then we'd get busy at reorganizing the cabin to accommodate four
people.

Now what to do with the chamber pot!

*March 8th*

At noon, the Cessna touched down on our snowshoed runway in front of
the cabin. Dorcas and Richard disembarked staggering under loads of
parcels, their faces bright with smiles.

Introductions and scrambling to unload all seemed to take place at the
same time. I was embarrassed to see that my comment about being self re-
liant had been taken quite literally. Included in their gear was a large
canvas tent complete with wood stove.

"You didn't have to bring accommodation along!"

"It'll give us all more privacy." said Richard pleasantly. I was grateful
for his easy response.

Over lunch we learned about Dorcas' experiences at the nursing
stations in remote settlements and Richard's work with the Canadian
Wildlife Service. Both are well acquainted with this part of the northern
wilderness. Dorcas is knowledgeable in native campcraft and Richard is a
dyed-in-the-wool naturalist.

As with most of our other visitors our apprehension about seeing people
seems silly already. Dorcas and Richard are in the early stages of a ro-
mance but after this holiday they will be separated for a while because of
job commitments. And we were fussing about our privacy when we have
another three months to enjoy alone in the valley!

Dorcas hasn't lost an ounce of her energy. When lunch was over she
popped up from the table to unpack the groceries they had brought in.
She produced everything from canned lobster, fresh fruit and vegetables
to a large roast of beef, explaining that they had practically bought out
the local grocery store in Watson Lake. I believed her!

*March 9th*

Gusting winds slapped the raw, cold air in our faces and tore through our clothing as we headed downriver on snowshoes. We got as far as the hotsprings but did not remain there long, the four of us reluctantly agreeing that it was one day we were better off spending closer to home. Back in camp, Richard took to the kitchen to bake bread while John busied himself with odd jobs. Dorcas and I went on a tour of the forests north of the cabin. She was keen on snaring snowshoe hares and I wanted to see how it was done.

Once a trail was located, Dorcas straddled it and suspended a wire noose from an alder branch that she bent over the tracks. A bounding hare would hang itself on the wire if it was positioned correctly, and Dorcas made several adjustments to ensure that the hare would run through, not under or to the side of the snare.

We returned home to announce that the snares were set, but the news fell on unsympathetic ears.

"You catch 'em, you skin 'em," Richard cautioned but Dorcas remained undaunted by the comment. As queasy as my stomach was at the thought of these beautiful creatures being thrown into a pot for stew, I admired Dorcas' spunk. If the snares worked I didn't doubt for a minute she would take to the task of skinning them without batting an eyelash.

*March 12th*

When the skies cleared we showed our guests our favorite landmarks. A snowshoe to the hotsprings, Big Island Lake and Bologna Creek gave them the lay of the land.

Today John and I went west from Snake Creek to break trail, and Richard and Dorcas went east, along our old portage trail. The plan was to meet again on the island at Big Island Lake. The route was about a four-mile circuit and would take us each an hour to pack down half of it.

We were trudging through knee high drifts, but the day was warm and sunny and we enjoyed the workout. We had brought our camera equipment, optimistic that animals would be stirring on this early spring day. Perhaps a moose would be browsing amongst the stunted trees. These docile creatures were always a treat to see. However, it was not a moose that caught our eye.

"Jo, see that small animal moving towards us?" John whispered. I nodded. I thought perhaps our marten friend had ventured further from home than the woods near the cabin.

We were downwind of the small dark form, so we crouched low and crept stealthily through the sparse timber. We advanced about fifty yards

*Snowshoeing up Three Bears*

before the animal stopped dead in its tracks. It peered around and then took a nosedive into a drift and disappeared. We dropped our packs on the spot, mounted the zoom lens, and waited.

The dark face popped up again, breaking the surface like a submarine's periscope. It had probably caught sight of our movement the first time, rather than our smell, for it seemed content to resume its journey. Only then did we see the creature's distinctive form of locomotion — it alternated between steps and slides. We had ourselves an otter!

Before trying to get closer, John took a couple of pictures. I held the camera while he moved towards the otter to force it into a dive. I wanted to catch a head-on picture when it emerged from the tunnel.

But the animal had other plans. It dove completely out of sight and after several unsuccessful attempts to uncover its escape route we abandoned the chase.

*March 13th*

This afternoon Richard showed us how to build a quincee — a snowhouse for wilderness survival.

He shovelled the snow out of a ten foot square area, removed the ground shrubs, then refilled the hole and made a six-foot-high dome into which he stuck several four-inch-long willow twigs.

He let it sit for three hours to sublimate (during which the snow converts from a solid state to vapour and solidifies again. There is no liquid state because the temperature is too cold to melt the snow.) He then gophered out the inside by hand. By removing only enough snow that the inside tips of the twigs were showing, he ensured an even wall depth of four inches.

As Dorcas and Richard plan to sleep in the snowhouse, they added the finishing touches — air holes and a thick bed of spruce boughs that provides warmth and reduces drafts by making the floor level higher than the entrance.

We had serious doubts about the quincee's solidness, so in the evening Richard invited us all to stand on it. The test convinced us. A moose could lumber over it without damaging it!

We watched our friends retire for the night. Once inside, Richard blocked off the entranceway with garbage bags filled with snow.

*March 15th*

You couldn't see the table for the food — bread, cheeses, fresh fruit, pan-

cakes and scrambled eggs, jams and honey. To wash it all down was cup
after cup of steaming hot coffee.

We snowshoed two miles upriver to the mouth of Bologna Creek, then
up the timbered slopes, down through forested valleys and along the edge
of the hundred-foot cliffs bordering the Bologna Creek Canyon. A light
snow was falling and the temperature had risen to minus ten.

By afternoon we descended into a shallow valley, well protected from
the winds, that we had already chosen as our base camp. The snowy white
bowl, studded with white and black spruce, was flat enough to accommodate our tents.

Setting up a proper base camp would take until nightfall, so we each assumed responsibility for one or more of the chores. No sooner were packs
peeled from our shoulders than we began to collect firewood, dig out a pit
for the fire, stamp out platforms for the tents, dig a privy, and collect
spruce boughs to lay beneath our ensolite pads and sleeping bags.

By nightfall we were changed into dry clothing, and every necessity for
keeping warm and well fed was within easy reach — inside the large firepit — on a shelf of packed snow and spruce boughs. The cold kept us close
to the blaze that was roaring at our feet, but after a day of constant motion
we were content to remain there while preparing a multi-course dinner.
Hot tea and soup, followed by freeze-dried chicken stew, bannock and
dessert was our reward.

Outside the large circular pit, the night air was clear, but the sting of
the cold was enough to nip noses and cheeks when we stood up to stretch.

A shrill wail came from a distant ridge. The wolves. Were they on the
hunt? It was the right time of the month. We caught glimpses of sparkling
jewels overhead and a full moon on the rise between fast moving clouds. If
the pack visited the cabin tonight they did so without an audience.

*March 16th*

We took turns breaking trail today — a tough exercise, because we were
venturing through country that even the animals stayed clear of — but
with four of us in the lineup we made decent headway. While travelling
through spruce forests and up the knolls and ridges, we marvelled at the
wind-swept peaks of the Ragged Range that loomed in the hazy horizon
to the southeast.

There seemed to be no life in the woods other than ourselves. Were all
the animals holed up beneath the white blanket or deep within the hollow
of some tree trunk?

Silence in a forest leads one to seek out life in what we are conditioned to think are lifeless things — drifts blown into fascinating configurations, a unique pattern in the snow, the different feel that one forest has from another, or the dramatic effect of a ray of sunlight streaming down the face of a mountain.

These are all part of the distinct presence one feels in a winter forest, the natural forces we know are at work but can't always see — like the wind as it quietly sails through the empty branches of frozen trees and skims over the snowbound forest floor. It is not fantasy, imagining that an invisible hand is at work, constantly moulding and carving. In a hushed forest on a still winter day one's own sensitivity makes a white, seemingly motionless setting, come alive.

*March 19th*

"The quiet rings in your ears," said John as we stood on the runway watching the Beaver bank into a turn and fly south through Bologna Creek Pass, carrying Richard and Dorcas back to civilization. Events flashed through my mind like cuts from a motion picture reel — the highlights of an active ten days.

John didn't understand the need I felt to go walking for a while and as I saddled on my snowshoes he remained silent — a sign he wasn't sure whether or not he liked the idea.

"You can come along you know."

"Thanks, but I'll pass."

"Okay then. I won't go farther than Bologna Creek. I'll be back in an hour."

He looked up from the gun cleaning chore he had thrown himself into. He has a tendency to keep his hands busy when doing his thinking.

"I'll be right here," he answered.

The day was a fine one — marvellously warm with the sunshine glistening off the snowy river surface like a spray of diamonds. I followed in our snowshoed trail, the crusted top so firm I fairly skidded along. My arms swung to and fro, in rhythm to the glide of my legs. As I gained momentum all thoughts of anything else faded.

The blast, followed by a ping, echoed across the river. I froze in midstride, absolutely stunned for several seconds before I came to my senses enough to realize what the noise was.

"The gun! That was the gun!" I cried out. John never fired our Lee Enfield without first announcing his intention to try a practice shot. The one horror that overwhelmed all sensible reasoning was that the .303 had accidentally fired when John was cleaning it. In a burst of speed, I turned for home and ran, my legs shaking and the tears welling up in my eyes.

"John!" I screamed when I reached the clearing. "John, answer me."

I didn't break stride until I was near the waterhole and then I called out again, my voice croaking and broken with gasps.

John came out of the cabin and walked down the path towards me. "Jo, what's wrong?"

My legs couldn't support me any longer. I threw my arms around his neck and sobbed.

"Why did you fire the gun?" I choked. "I thought you were hurt."

I was too relieved to do anything else but cry.

*March 28th*

Spring was some four weeks ahead of schedule at the hotsprings, we learned, when the day broke gloriously sunny and mild and we took to the frozen river on skis. Not a trace of snow remained on the silty beaches that banked the tepid stream, and grass and new plantlife were already in evidence.

The warm water feeding into the South Nahanni was extending the boundary of open water. Breakup was in its advanced stages. Floating ice sheets, some a foot thick, ricocheted off the banks of the opposite shore and bumped their way through the narrow channel of open water. The rushing water foamed at our feet and spattered over the rock beds. We had to yell to hear each other over the din. The spring breakup of bubbling creeks back home is tame compared to this.

We had followed wolf tracks on our downriver ski to the springs, but at the sandy beach they were lost in the jumble of other tracks. We picked them up again along the rocky north shore past the merging point of the springs and the river. From the freshness of the tracks it appeared we were not far behind the pack. Rounding a bend we were surprised witnesses to a rare sight.

"Look, wolves on the rim ice ahead." A pack of a dozen wolves was playing on the frozen surface of the opposite shore. They continued their frolic quite unaware of our presence, but it was only a matter of time before our scent would be carried on the wind towards them.

"Hey! There's a moose on our shore across from them." John exclaimed. He handed me the zoom lens and pointed. No more than fifty yards downriver the forlorn creature stood steadfast, probably mystified by the combination of man scent and the sight of the wolves.

Wolves and moose scattered in opposite directions. What might have been a fatal encounter for the moose was halted by our arrival.

Were the wolves attempting to lead the moose onto the open stretch of snow-covered ice? We had read that this tactic is often employed to take down a hoofed animal, moose or caribou. Hooves have no gripping power on a slippery surface, and the wolves can outrun and outmanoeuvre their prey. Although one moose can kill a wolf with a flash of his powerful legs, or fend off an attack using his antlers, the sheer numbers in a pack and the wolves' ability to work as a team make it easy prey.

*March 31st*
Avalanches! We saw the first one of the season on one of the steepest slopes of the Bologna Range. The loud crack seemed to resonate from the lower part of the canyon, but the thunderous roar that followed minutes later came from a cleft in the mountain — high up where the mountain goats roamed in a barren wasteland of rock and snow. We saw a puff of snowy mist and then the white sheet sliding down the face with incredible speed. It was a sure sign of spring's advance.

*April 1st*
During the latter part of March there was a dramatic shift in the weather. A balmy wind, sailing in from the west, blew for three days, bringing with it a spread of thunderclouds that yielded not snow but rain. Aside from the inconvenience of a leaky woodshed roof we were not bothered by this latest turn of events. The warmer air and precipitation melted much of the surrounding snow and the best, we hoped, was yet to come. If the temperature went back down to the subzero mark, we would have a glazed surface and a healthy crust of snow or ice — superb conditions for walking.

The thermometer dropped to minus ten, exactly as we had hoped. We could now snowshoe up mountains without breaking through the crust into powdery snow up to our thighs.

Our first outing was cut short by a nasty fog that shrouded all but the base of the Three Bears in a thick cloak of mist. We had made camp halfway up the mountain, but when we awoke in the morning visibility was less than fifty yards, so we returned home to wait out the system.

Shafts of sunlight streamed through the cabin windows and woke us on this Sunday "fool's day" — the break we were waiting for. By afternoon, we were traversing the slope of the Three Bears again, with food enough for four days and sufficient clothing to fend off even the coldest of mountain temperatures. The single addition to the outfit was a ski pole each to help provide traction on the firmed up snow surface. Some sections were so steep and slippery we sidestepped our way up, digging the edges of our snowshoes into the crust while pulling ourselves up on the poles. We were in camp before dark. Tent, equipment, and the food cache were as we had left them with no signs that animals had sniffed about.

When enough dry wood was gathered and sawed into one-foot lengths, we arranged our ensolite pads on the bough covered snow shelves around the outside edge of the firepit. A pot of snow hung from a dingle stick over the crackling blaze (a notched or hooked branch, preferably green and free of foliage, placed at the edge of the fire pit at a slight angle so that a pot of water can hang from it), and as we waited for our tea water to boil, we stared out over the ice walls enclosing us at the fiery colours of the setting sun. The mountain tops were backlighted in shades of yellow-green and rose.

### April 2nd

We broke camp early after a cold restless night. Our fingers and toes were still stiff with cold and I was dazed from too little sleep.

For the first two hundred feet of climb we had quite a workout, as there was no film of ice on the surface. With each step the lead person was ploughing through three and a half feet of powder. When it had rained around the cabin in late March, it must have been snowing in the mountains.

At timberline a complete change of clothing was necessary. Down parkas were replaced by sweaters, vests and windbreakers. For the first time this year we put on some tanning lotion. The final stretch was more than a thousand-foot climb on hard packed, windblown snow.

As we climbed higher we had a better view of the face of the mountain. The slope alternated between ridges of rock outcroppings and snowslide routes. One strip we had to cross was as smooth as a paved highway. It would be treacherous because any false move might set off a snowslide.

Before negotiating this hazard, we each tied fifty feet of bright yellow rope around our waists. Should one of us get carried away down a slide, the rope would serve as a guide for the rescuer. During the crossing we put distance between ourselves and kept a watchful eye upwards.

John climbed ahead while I remained behind to watch for snowslides, then he watched while I made the ascent.

We traversed the crucial section without incident and rested in the lee of three immense rocks. The remainder of the climb would be made without snowshoes, because the ridge was too narrow for anything but hiking boots.

Our route now was right along the crown of the ridge, where the foot-

*Joanne investigates wolf body prints on snow*

ing was rock or ice. We had to force ourselves not to look behind or to either side, where the rockface fell off at an eighty degree angle. One misplaced foothold or a blast of wind would be disastrous.

When we looked straight up we saw that the summit was much closer than we had thought, but the danger lay in the cornice. The prevailing winds from the south had swept the snow over the rim of the mountain top and the drifts had curled back under. We found a spot where we would not have to break through the gigantic frozen wave of snow and risk being thrown off balance, but to reach it we had to make a vertical climb.

We held a short strategy session. John would go first, and should he trigger an avalanche he was to "swim" with the flow to keep on top. Trying to move clear of the path of a slide would be fruitless. In the event of trouble, I would have to act as rescuer.

By digging into the hard snow wall with the toe of his boot, John was able to carve out hand and footholds. He advanced upward as though climbing a ladder. When I heard the faint "Come on up!" I made the final hundred feet as he had and joined him on the summit.

The windchill factor made it deathly cold up top, but I have never seen anything so spectacular. Bordering the vast tract of snowfield we stood on were several pure white domes and to the south more peaks, so snow-coated that their lines were almost obliterated. Shallow depressions between the lofty mounds marked gulleys and gorges. To the east was sheep country, the Sawtooth Mountains — jagged, free of snow for the most part, and foreboding. To the west lay the Bologna Ridge, the upper valley, and, more than sixty miles distant in a haze of pink light, the Northwest Territory-Yukon divide and the pyramid-shaped Mount Wilson.

The day's climb was the riskiest we had tried, but the reward of seeing our valley from this vantage point was the most marvellous high we had ever experienced.

### April 8th

We were up with the sun to pack for a long cross-country ski upriver. We have become very efficient at the routine of packing and unpacking our gear.

Our supplies for camping are almost standard. Emergency equipment like repair-and first-aid kits is never unpacked. Clothing changes with the seasons, but the cold weather extras are always added in case the weather takes a turn for the worse. Even our menus remain unaltered, but when you've only got six basic dinner foods to choose from, life is pretty simple. The day hot buttered bannock with strawberry jam did not taste absolutely scrumptious was a day that we hadn't worked hard enough. After a ten-mile hike and two hours setting up camp, any food cooked over an open fire is a delicacy.

By midafternoon we were some ten miles from the cabin. The temperature had soared, turning the snow into wet slush that was matting along the length of our skis. It was, as John put it, "a klister afternoon" (a warm weather wax for cross-country skiing), and unfortunately we were klister-less. Our pace slowed to a tedious crawl.

We sought out a campsite where dead wood was plentiful and we could view sunrise and sunset. We found what we wanted in an old burn area where dry, charred spruce stood amongst the new pine growth — a winter camper's dream.

While setting up camp we were entertained by the antics of a hawk owl. The medium-sized day hunter, with piercing yellow eyes, was perched twenty feet up on the tip of a large spruce when we spotted him. His "kikikikikiki" high-pitched call made him easy to detect. A bloodstained hind quarter of a snowshoe hare was clutched tightly in his claws.

Later, as I hunched over the fire to tend to our homemade stew and dumplings, the sound of flapping and terrified screeches filled the clearing. We had front row seats at an amazing drama. The owl, pumping his wings with such force that we could almost feel the vibration, chased a small bird through the trees. The victim was swooping up and down and side to side — manoeuvres that would have done credit to a fighter pilot, but the owl was equally skilful. The strike was made quickly and cleanly.

Darkness fell soon after with the low rumble of avalanches sounding on the night air. We settled back in comfort on the snow ledge, in front of the fire.

*April 9th*

When we shuffled ourselves out of the tent, we saw evidence of nocturnal visitors. Wolves again! But this time, the barrier between us and one of the pack members was not seven inches of log wall but the flimsy nylon of a tent.

We were glad we had cached the food before we turned in. Even the wet clothing that was hung on a tripod-supported pole over the firepit had been taken down — a wise move given the proven palate of wolves.

As we investigated the paw prints in the snow we became increasingly miffed at how our guest had moved about the tent area so silently. There were several gaping holes in the snow where the wolf had broken through — surely he must have made some noise? Were we sleeping that soundly? We were about five miles along our route when we saw twenty-five neat impressions in the snow, where each wolf had lain to rest. Their body outlines and even facial features were clearly distinguishable. Dirt from the animals' coats was embedded in the snow making it easy to determine sizes and shapes. All, it seemed, were well fed; their bodies, especially their trunks and haunches, were thickset.

We had stopped for lunch when we saw what looked like a rib cage lying on the ice in the middle of the river. Closer inspection verifed our hunch — the backbone and ribs of what had once been a moose were picked clean. The markings in the snow showed it had been chased out onto the river and brought down there.

The afternoon sun was blazing hot. Our faces were sunburnt, our lips chapped and, even with sunglasses on, our eyes were smarting. Patches of green were showing on the river where the surface had been a solid white strip earlier in the day. It was time to begin the ski back to camp. The river ice was melting.

*April 12th*

We can longer delay the chore neither of us is looking forward to — packing to leave the cabin. It is depressing even to consider that our days in the valley are numbered, and we would further delay the inevitable had a recent development not made procrastination impossible.

In August, Welcome North Mines discovered a lode of lead-zinc on the mountain opposite our cabin, after a summer of mineral exploration. Diamond drilling was to begin soon after the spring thaw. In a few days, a pilot from B.C. Yukon will begin flying in fuel to Big Island Lake. The Otter, we've learned, will be making several trips between Tungsten and the lake, and on each flight out the plane will be empty. We can take advantage of this to have our extra supplies flown out to Watson Lake. Otherwise we will have to leave them here until after our canoe trip down the South Nahanni, then charter a plane to return us to the cabin after we reach Watson Lake.

We began organizing our belongings and packing what we wouldn't need on the river — but not without many nostalgic interruptions.

The cabin was stripped of everything we could live without, including the two-way radio. Clothing, cooking and eating utensils, some books and other equipment we'd need for camping were all that remained. The rest was packed up and labelled just as carefully as it had been some twelve months earlier, when the wilderness life was still just a dream.

# A Sorrowful Departure

The long days (sunrise at eight and sunset at seven) and the ten degree average temperatures made hikes on snowshoes or skis a morning ritual. Our well worn river paths still served as access routes to places we had not yet explored. We could travel for ten or more miles upriver and then break off into the forests along the south bank, where the mountains blocked the sun and the thaw was slower. As long as we set out before dawn, when the air temperature was below freezing and returned before the sun rose too high, we could go wherever we wanted.

The path to Big Island Lake and points north was still firm, and we took advantage of this when Pine Tree Mountain began to shed its winter coat. Of the miles of wilderness we tracked, it was morning hikes up the earth spotted face of Pine Tree that most vividly brought to life the miraculous beauty of these spring days.

The grey jays, all plump from overeating, twittered happily from treetop to treetop, following us for hours as if they had nothing more pressing to do. Their unending monologues blended naturally with the buzz of the wakening forests and the sheer exuberance we felt ourselves.

The red squirrels, out from their winter dens, were scurrying over the icy surface of snow with large dried mushrooms hanging from their jaws or clasped between tiny front paws — the last of their winter cache stores. Rambunctious hares, their coats turning spotted and grey, darted in and out of the maze of shrubs, heedless of the heavy loads of snow they dislodged from the elbows of higher branches. Rays of sunlight, filtering through overhanging boughs, spotlighted bursts of colour — patches of lime-green step moss and moisture-laden earth around the bases of the large spruce. The pungent aroma of wet soil and sodden, decaying leaves permeated the air.

Occasionally, my eye would wander over a clump of bushes where shrivelled up rose hips clung defiantly to a branch. The tinge of red was a reminder that ripe fruit would soon dot the forest greenery.

The spruce grouse, in the early stages of their mating performance,

*Spruce grouse*

were perfectly camouflaged, their feathered bodies matching in colour and texture the partially snow-blanketed ground and squat bushes. We could hear their drumming, but only when they bobbed out from behind the screen of browns and greens could we watch them closely. Then, as their "fool hen" nickname suggests, they would remain in full view for the longest time — the perfect target for the camera.

If there was ever a formula for being truly happy, these wandering moments provided it. Springtime in mountainous country is one of Nature's most dramatic seasons — when the first blue streak of open water heralds changes on the river, when the flocks of mergansers and buffleheads once more cruise atop the wind rippled surface of Snake Creek, and when the first bear prints on the corn textured snow told us that the bruins were once again on the move. We were witness to, and spiritually very much part of, the most sensuous of the four northern seasons.

*Easter Sunday*

We have drawn up a six week menu for our three hundred mile canoe trip to Nahanni Butte. Many of its ingredients, such as easy-to-cook freeze-dried dinners, were stored away in midwinter. As the date of departure nears, rationing is getting tight, because it seems better to save as many luxuries as possible for our active canoeing days. Among the things we are temporarily doing without are cooking oil, raisins, peanuts, margarine, peanut butter, jam, pancake mix and eggs. And our supply of flour and sugar is tiny.

Baking now demands sheer genius in order to come up with appetizing meals that provide enough food energy to fuel our many hikes. Soups thickened with freeze-dried vegetables and muffins held together with the smallest amount of flour have become mainstays. I double the quantities of powdered milk or either bran or cornmeal in the biscuits, so they at least look as if they have some bulk to them. Lard is now our chief source of fat. We are much leaner than in midwinter, when we tried to put weight on to fend off the cold.

The reduced quantity of sugar in our diet seems to affect our temperaments too. We move less quickly, as if our bodies are warning us to conserve whatever energy foods we consume. Despite this, and the fact that we have become grotesquely thin, we feel supremely healthy!

Today we rose before dawn, so the additional time needed to concoct breakfast would not cut into our skiing. I spent yesterday evening trying to figure out how to produce an Easter treat from the few staples we have left. The result is steamed Boston Brown Bread, cut up and fried in lard and dressed very frugally with peach jam. The objective was to try to hide the fact that we are eating cornmeal again. Johnnycake, cornmeal pancakes, and muffins have become increasingly unpopular with John, to the point where anything baked that tastes mealy or even hints at a golden colour almost turns his stomach.

He managed to put away three-quarters of the loaf, showing no signs that he suspected the ingredients. He downed an inordinate amount of orange juice with each bite, but I shrugged this off, thinking our decreased allowance of coffee (down to one small cup a meal from six) was the cause.

Another unusual thing about this Easter is that we have never been so sensitive to the religious significance of the day. We spent many evenings reflecting on the words written in the Bible, especially the Scripture readings concerning the death of Christ. Good Friday was a sombre day in the cabin, Saturday somewhat the same, and today, the minute we rose, we acted as if we had just been released from a lengthy period of confinement. For the two of us to ponder so seriously the reasons for what we believe is unusual, but where better than here, where we feel so close to the workings of the Creator.

*April 24th*
The quiet of the valley is to be interrupted for a few days while the B.C. Yukon Air Service ferries more than two hundred drums of gasoline into Big Island Lake. It's a disturbing thought that the wilderness John and I have grown so much a part of will never be quite the same.

"The canoeists this summer are going to be disgusted when they see those helicopters swarming around," I said. "I can imagine what our spot will look like in five or six years."

My dream of returning to the South Nahanni some years down the road was quickly losing its appeal. I knew I could forget any notions of seeing the valley the way it was. Patterson's comment about seeing the South Nahanni at its best in '28-29 seemed truer than ever.

The sound of an airplane coming through Bologna Creek Pass confirmed my feelings. The pilot, Byron, unloaded a skidoo, a trailer and a windsock, looking very businesslike and saying little to us. We managed to get a bit of information from him about the mining company's plans. When he said there was some talk about our cabin being used as a cookhouse for the summer I turned silent. The one thing I did not want our cabin used for was a base for a mining camp. I had hoped it would house canoeists overnight! John gave me an understanding glance and I calmed down. After all, Bryon wasn't responsible for this newest development; he was

*John looking down on the South Nahanni and Ragged Range*

just doing his job. I'd wait, I thought to myself, and vent my anger on a log.

We confirmed arrangements for our supplies to be flown out on one of the runs and returned to the cabin to check the equipment one more time before loading it onto our sled and Crazy Carpet.

*April 29th*

We made several trips between the lake and cabin, to coincide with Byron's hourly trips. The tireless pilot performed like a work horse. He was in the air some fourteen hours a day and on each landing he stopped only long enough to assist his helper, Ray, unload the drums onto the ice, from where they would be moved by skidoo onto higher land.

The lake ice was mostly slush and puddles of water when we returned after dinner to load our two hundred and fifty pounds of packages into the empty plane.

"We'll store these boxes in the hangar for you," he promised. "When do you hope to be in Watson Lake anyway?"

This was a question we were unable to answer. So much depended on the river conditions. Bologna Creek was open, but the South Nahanni remained frozen enough to walk on. Breakup was going to proceed slowly, over several weeks, not in one tremendous explosion of water and ice chunks as we had hoped.

"If the ice just rots away, we could still be at the cabin past the middle of May. That would mean arriving at the Butte sometime in late June and Watson Lake maybe a week later, depending on flight arrangements," I said.

"It depends on high water too," John added. "We won't shoot through the Four Canyons in floodtime so we might have to sit off the river for a week or so. We could be in town as early as June 1st if we're on the water within ten days."

Byron told us what he had seen from the air. "Water's open in spots above Bologna Creek. It could be two weeks before all the ice goes out, could be longer. Depends on the weather."

Having learned the northerners' way of dealing with matters beyond their control John responded in true sourdough fashion. "We'll see you when we get there."

With that bit of profundity, we waved Byron off and waited until the Otter slipped into the pass before we headed down the path for home.

The setting sun was a ball of red flame suspended over the rim of the jagged western horizon when we slid down the hill onto Snake Creek and hurriedly made our way across the wet marshland. "This could be our last snowshoe over the creek," I said dispiritedly. The pools of melted snow had grown in the last few days, from mere puddles on the ice to deep wells of black water. It was becoming increasingly dangerous to be out walking around.

As we crossed the sunlit marsh, I wondered if the memories of such moments as these could possibly be kept alive.

*May 1st*
Darkness now found us groping around the cabin without any light (the lanterns sat in Watson Lake). Card games around the nightly bonfire were our single form of entertainment. Cribbage was fast losing its appeal, as the running total of games we each won will verify (Joanne 172, John 186). This left Honeymoon Bridge and, as a last resort, Solitaire. We were doggedly determined not to pick up the two novels that now comprised our library, because these were earmarked for rainy day reading on the river.

The return of the wolves this evening banished all thoughts of boredom.

In response to the choir of deep-throated howls echoing from the forest near Snake Creek, John grabbed the rifle and camera without saying a word.

This time even I was anxious to get moving for fear we might miss something. For almost the first time I felt excitement and not fear.

When we broke out of the treed area, the last of the long orange shadows of sunset bathed the marsh. Landmarks were still distinguishable, but not for long — the last splurge of colour soon faded behind the wall of mountains. There was not a wolf in sight when we first scanned the borders of the creek and unless something materialized soon, we would be engulfed in darkness.

"Do you see any snow on the rim of that hill?" John whispered, pointing to two spots directly in front of where we sat, no more than twenty yards away.

"Yes, there's two blobs at the edge...just a little to our right."

"Those blobs are wolves."

I grabbed the fieldglasses and sure enough focused on two silver wolves. Both stood upright and still, except for their heads, which swayed back and forth, back and forth.

Two wolves could not have made voice with the volume we had heard and as seconds passed I began to get scared. Where were the rest? Why was I suddenly feeling that we were being surrounded?

"Let's get out of here, " I urged John,

No sooner had I said it than the pack appeared, one by one, across the top of the cutbank. The two silver wolves stood guard while twenty-six others passed between them, heading west. Some of the pack voiced mild to enthusiastic acknowledgements as they trotted by, others remained silent. Only when the entire pack was out of sight did the guards move on. It was one of the most organized performances we had witnessed since first encountering these incredible animals.

As if in a final gesture, to make it clear to us who was watching who, a single wolf, its brown coat shaggy and unkempt, materialized out of thin air and moved casually down the treed embankment to the valley floor. Once at our level, it stopped, glared directly at us, barked as a dog would at a passing stranger, and then departed.

*May 9th*

The urge to remain in the valley longer but at the same time to get moving is a difficult feeling to explain. The trauma of saying goodbye to our first home, one built with our own hands, is offset by a compulsion to see what lies beyond the blue haze of the mountains called the Mackenzies.

For more than a week we have repeated the same routine, beginning with the morning question: "Any change?" the answer to which is always, "No, not out front, but let's take a walk before breakfast." Then we walk down to the end of the bare patch of ground in front of the cabin and address ourselves to the solid block of ice covering the river.

"Break up!" John would implore.

Downriver, sheets of the ice shelf were melting and breaking off from the edges of the main block. This process had started about four weeks before, beginning at the hotsprings, and was gradually proceeding toward us. The river was fairly navigable for a distance below the hotsprings, but whether the open conditions extended five, ten or twenty miles beyond that point was anyone's guess.

We returned home from the morning's river patrol more impatient and fidgety than usual. If we stay here much longer we will have to dig into the food supplies for downriver. The tally of remaining rations is five meals of spaghetti noodles, two packages of baking soda, a cup of rice, a cup of oatmeal and eight ounces of powdered milk. A can of ham, a bag of freeze-dried green beans and a serving each of instant potatoes have been set aside for our last night in the cabin.

I suggested that we organize a grouse hunt to supplement our larder. When Dwight last dropped in he left us a slingshot to hunt small game. After my lesson in using this basic weapon we had shelved the idea of seriously hunting with it. But given the sorry state of our cupboards it no longer seemed a bad idea.

The decision made, we scavenged the beaches for perfectly round stones to use as ammunition. We were laughing when we returned to the cabin with our tattered green army pants sagging under the weight of the stones in our pockets.

"The grouse will hear me coming before they see me." I said, and as I caught a reflection of myself in the large kitchen window I snickered at how I looked. Apart from my baggy pants with the bulging side and back pockets, I was swimming in one of John's gingham shirts and my hair was piled up under a grimy old fishing cap. The figure looking back at me in the glass needed only a pole fishing rod slung over the shoulder to complete the Tom Sawyer image.

John was already heading along the path through the forest, so I quickened my step to catch up to him, enjoying my private chuckle and thinking I should get a picture of the two of us. From the hind end, John resembled a tired old packhorse, waddling down the trail on its last legs.

For three frustrating hours we tramped through the bush on the lookout for defenceless grouse.

We saw several perched on tree branches or bobbing through the undergrowth. Those on the move were in no danger of injury with either of us behind the slingshot. After a couple of close calls, when we nearly ran into trees trying to follow them and aim at the same time, we became more selective in choosing which of the birds to shoot at. Those well camouflaged and sitting motionless on the spruce boughs were harder to find but safer to aim at. But even the stationary targets had little to fear from us. At the instant I released a stone my hand would tremble or shift slightly and my missile would mortally wound a twig or a clump of earth. John's coaching at the sidelines was little help.

"That one was wide," he whispered. I set another stone in the rubber strap, took aim and fired again. The stone shot clear over the spruce top.

Impatient with me, John took over, but with no better results.

The confused bird just sat there while we repeatedly reset the sling and fired. These birds weren't just defenceless, they were stupid. If we caught a pair of them together, one frozen on a branch while our small pellets flew in all directions, its mate perched nearby obstinately refused to move as well.

We continued the hunt for a few more fruitless rounds before slinking home in embarrassment. Our prey had obviously not heard about sitting ducks.

The time had come to reevaluate our original plan of waiting for the river to break up in front of the cabin before leaving for the Butte. I waited until we were back home before I voiced my feelings, hoping John would be more responsive after our failure to secure fresh meat for camp. When the time seemed right, I broached the subject of leaving early.

"I've written our choices on either side of this cardboard. One reads 'wait until the river breaks up' and the other, 'leave tomorrow.' The best out of five flips we act on."

"I don't know Jo. It seems a drastic move."

"What's drastic about it?" I prodded, knowing full well what he meant.

"Well..."

"Well?" I urged.

"Well... Oh, okay. We'll do it your way."

When two out of three flips came up "leave tomorrow" John looked as though he would like to back down, but I insisted that he stick to his word, If the "leave tomorrow" came up again, we would spend the rest of the day packing.

And it did!

"Huh boy!" was John's exasperated response.

"Look, we know a spring run on this river is going to be tricky whether we put into open water a mile from here tomorrow or set off from home shore a week from now. If the conditions are worse than we expect, we'll sit off the river for a day to two, but at least we'll be in new country. We've been sitting idle for over a week and I don't want to remember our final days here like that. Doesn't that make sense, John?" It must have. The corners of his mouth turned up slightly in a grin and his moustache twitched. Then he jumped up from the table and began hauling sacks out of the rafters. "Let's pack then," he laughed.

*May 10th*

We awoke to three degrees and dull skies. The rain that had teemed down during the night had stopped, but a low ceiling of turgid grey cloud blocked the sun.

After breakfast — a dandy because we had dug into our supplies for the trip downriver and unearthed a ration of pancakes and eggs — John piled our supplies on the picnic table while I swept the cabin floor.

We pegged the shutters in place and then stood together in the centre of the room. The cabin looked bare and cold. The note we had mounted on the wall said everything.

Our stay here at the Island Lakes has been truly enjoyable. Working together, we built this cabin, cut firewood and blazed trails to neighborhood sites. We've hiked, canoed, skiied and snowshoed up and down the valley and into the mountains through four glorious seasons.

We leave this cabin now and hope that it will offer refuge to future travellers. Please remember that others will follow. Kindling near the stove and a few scoops of cold ashes in the kybo will be duly appreciated. Check the stovepipes before lighting a fire, and put the shutters up when you leave. We have left some supplies in the cache — use them if in need.

As newlyweds, we spent twelve months in Nahanni country and feel enriched by the experience. We found a special peace here and hope you do as well.

Today we leave for Nahanni Butte in our Grumman canoe with six weeks of supplies. Wherever your trailhead or trailend lies, we wish you a safe and happy journey.

# Days On The River

The crown of Snow White emerged from the low cloud cover just as we positioned ourselves fore and aft of the Grumman. John had a leather strap across his forehead with a line of rope attached to it so he could pull from the front. I shoved the overloaded canoe from behind. Grunting with each step, we inched our way forward over the snow. A strong wind that drove the pillows of vapour into swirls around the peaks of the Ragged Range, worked wonders on the day's ominous weather. By the time we reached open water, a blue sky stretched above. The blazing sun turned the whole of the snow encrusted river that lay behind us into a glittering ribbon, so brilliant it made our eyes smart. Our wish for fair weather had been granted and we bid our homeground farewell, cheered by the prospect of a sunny afternoon.

All along the snowlined banks of the river were squawking ducks (mergansers, buffleheads and mallards), honking Canada geese, and antlerless moose, watching us as we sailed along.

At the hotsprings we bathed, then took a final walk inland, to the meadow, before shoving off into the fast moving current. There was no turning back now — just new country ahead waiting for the first two travellers of the season.

We were not familiar with the river below the springs. We had often said we would make up for this on our trip out, but as the twelve knot current sped us eastward we found we had to concentrate on the river conditions and were unable to devote more than fleeting glances to the surrounding mountains.

We floated through a winding, constricted channel that leaned to one side of the river. Some sections of this open strip were no wider than one yard, others varied from a few yards to twenty-five yards wide. Bobbing chunks of ice made the route hazardous. I had the fieldglasses ready at all times, so I could scout ahead for the best route. Rounding sharp turns we couldn't see until the last second whether the passageway was wide enough, or deep enough, for us to get through.

*Hauling the canoe to the hotsprings*

By evening, Snow White was miles away and out of sight. We chose a campsite on the lower end of a sandbar almost hugging the base of Big Red and in an ideal location to catch the last of the evening light and the first rays of dawn.

Just minutes before, we had negotiated a treacherous piece of water that at any other time of the year we would have avoided altogether by leaning to the right bank. The safer channel was still frozen, so we were forced to guide our craft around two half-submerged rocks and through a narrow stretch of large, standing waves. It was a brief but thrilling run through whitewater, and when we found ourselves able to relax again, we discovered we had had an audience — a large herd of caribou milling around on the north shore, a short distance away.

To float right up to the herd would almost certainly send the animals running, so we tried to slip around the south channel of an island directly ahead, with the hope of catching them off guard. But our stealthy approach was for naught. There wasn't a caribou to be seen when we broke into the main channel again.

Unlike the hundreds of canoeists who pass through this wilderness, we were travelling at the best time to observe game. The caribou were on their way to their summer feeding grounds, and the moose were once more roaming the valley's floor. For most of the valley's four-legged residents the river was now the main watering hole, and we were here in the middle of it. The knowledge that I was experiencing something few had shared gave me a tingling sensation that surpassed even the excitement of being on the move.

Eight months of silence had passed since last year's canoeists had run the river. This made us unexpected intruders, and we decided to take full advantage of the element of surprise by getting on the water early each morning and travelling as quietly as was humanly possible.

After we retired to the tent and again at dawn the next morning, we were roused from our beds by splashing sounds and the click of hooves — more small herds of caribou crossing the river. The whiff of smoke drifting from our fire and our stumbling to get out of the tent was enough to make these timid creatures retreat to the safety of the dark forest.

Within an hour of breaking camp, we encountered the first major set of rapids — water frothing around a maze of rocks that stretched across the width of open water and extended downstream for a good mile. We had no choice but to drive through this heaving cauldron, made even more dangerous by the number of ice floes speeding downriver out of control or spinning around in circles in the eddies.

We powered our craft forward through the foam, past the rocks and around the path of ice blocks — John screaming out commands and I searching the water in front of the bow while paddling, on the lookout for submerged rocks. In less than two minutes the whitewater was behind us and we could breath easily again.

We rounded a wide bend in the river, the second of two that show on a map of the South Nahanni River as an elongated, sideways S. As you travel southeastward down this stretch of the river, the eastern wall of the Ragged Range, rising abruptly from the water's edge, flanks you on the right; to the left, in the distance, are the magnificent Mackenzies, clothed in velvet-textured green forests and topped with a layer of snow.

Taking the turn was like emerging from an obstacle course onto a wide, calm boulevard. We now had more room to manoeuvre around the ice floes, but we should have realized the slack current was a warning of different conditions.

The first sign of trouble ahead was a conglomeration of ice slabs, piled one atop the other, across the width of the river. We gently nosed our bow in between one of the slabs and the shore ice, then climbed onto the ice to scout the hazard. There were two options open to us: wade back upstream to find a campsite, or push forward somehow and make camp at the first suitable place we came to.

We decided to try going on. The immediate objective was a large pool at the end of a very narrow channel. Beyond that was an open strip along the cliff-lined east bank, then some ice blocks and, finally, open water. If necessary we could slide the canoe over the ice for part of the way.

We made it through the channel, but the ice around the pool was too thick to break through and too weak in spots to walk on. We elected to head for shore and camp on the ice-coated gravel beach.

We paddled back to the midway point of the pool and ran the bow of the canoe up onto the ice shelf. The distance to shore was only a few yards, but we didn't have the leverage to slide the canoe forward using the paddles as poles. John cautiously stepped onto the ice and began pulling us forward. The canoe slid a few inches, and stopped.

To lighten the load, I stepped onto the ice, and together we dragged our craft towards shore.

Without warning, John went down — through the ice and into the blackest water I have ever seen.

The look of horror on his face as he floundered about in the frigid water terrified me so much I didn't think of what I was doing. I simply had to help him. Before he could yell at me to stop, I reached out for him — and down I went too.

For an instant I felt only numb fear and the gripping cold, then a wave

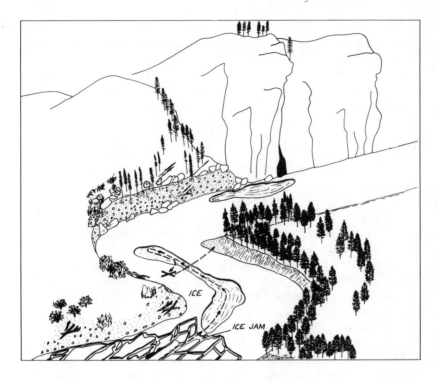

of shock passed through every part of me. I gasped for air and tried to scream, but no sound came. It was almost as if some person outside my body was doing all these things — the flailing arms and the spasmodic scramble to lift myself onto the ice. It didn't seem real.

Fragments of ice kept breaking off when I tried to support myself on the shelf. Plunging up to my shoulders in the cold water after each attempt, I wanted to cry out, but I was too frightened and numb.

After several attempts, John literally threw himself out of the water. Staying flat on his belly, he crawled to the canoe and flung a leg over the gunwale, then an arm. I grabbed his extended arm and he slowly dragged me out.

There wasn't a second to spare. As soon as the cold air hit our sodden bodies the numbness spread.

"Jo, listen to me," John gasped. "Paddle, okay? Paddle as hard as you can." He pointed to the treed bank.

The next few minutes were a blur of frenzied activity, powered by a strong will to survive. By some miracle, we succeeded in doing what only moments before had seemed impossible — we shoved the canoe forward over the ice using only our paddles.

Once on shore, John rifled throught the equipment pack for a bottle of fuel. He threw it to me and yelled at me to start a fire.

Stumbling forward, my drooping pants legs getting caught on the alder branches and weariness descending on me from the shock and the cold, I made it through the dense timber out onto a beach. I didn't have the strength to gather armloads of the driftwood lying around, so I drenched the first large stump I saw with Coleman fuel. When I set a match to it the gas exploded, igniting the tree and shooting out orange flames and blasts of heat. By the time I had stripped my clothes off, John was back with dry things for both of us and without saying a word we huddled close to the fire. Struck for an instant with the narrowness of our escape, I felt sick and had to force the thought from my mind. I stared blankly at the flames, thanking God we were both safe.

The following day we were back on the river, but only after a morning off to do some scouting from a higher elevation. We put into open water a short distance downstream from the beach and crossed to the opposite shore. We climbed a ridge, from where we could see for miles downriver to the convergence of the Nahanni and Broken Skull rivers.

The way looked clear. There was some back up of ice where the current slackened around bends, but through the fieldglasses the channel looked wide enough to direct the canoe through.

*Canada goose*

*Wolverine*

The sidetrip relieved some of the tension we felt from the previous day's close shave, but the anguish that our error in judgement cost us was not easily forgotten. I was subdued, convinced that John thought I was an idiot who didn't know the first thing about safety in or out of a canoe. Why I moved toward him on the ice I'll never know — a temporary leave of my senses I guess, coupled with the horrible shock of seeing a loved one in trouble. John felt deeply ashamed for not acting more sensibly and thus avoiding the near tragedy in the first place. The incident was a blow to his pride and self-confidence.

We set up camp next to a wide creek bed, in a lovely grove of pine and spruce. We were sitting, contented, watching the sun set when John flew off the stump he was seated on and dove for the gun.

"Grizzly!" he exclaimed.

The bear was less than ten yards from us, slightly raised on its hind legs, its dark brown coat in sharp contrast to the light buff colouring of its chest. The hump in its shoulders and the white tips of the hairs on its back were conclusive evidence. It was indeed a grizzly, joining us for dinner.

The standoff lasted only a moment. With its tail between its legs the intruder swiftly clambered up the mountainside.

The grizzly's bumbling entrance and masterfully executed retreat had all happened so quickly we hardly knew what to say. I was grateful, however, for the startled animal's reaction to us and its ability to remove itself without destroying our camp. From what I had gathered from reading Andy Russell's Grizzly Country, there is no more precarious position for a human than on the trail of a grizzly. And that's exactly where we had been. The tracks of our fleet-footed visitor showed that it had been walking along the sandy beach on the opposite side of the creek bed before it climbed the embankment and caught our scent.

If the bear had chosen to continue its evening stroll along the shore the only obstacles were two bodies, a fire and a tent — mere stepping stones.

"That's two close calls in two days Jo!"

"I'll pass on a third."

That night, the rumble of ice grinding along the shore was intermixed with a downpour and the low chatter of water running over the bed of stones next to our tent. I was up half the night wondering how safe our cached food was and whether the grizzly would return. The cracks of thunder rolling across the sky and the flashes of lightning that lit up the tent like a neon sign turned my insides into jelly. The affair over dinner did not seem to me to qualify as a "real encounter" with a grizzly. Were we in for another? I racked my brain trying to remember Andy Russell's words and whether or not these animals sought revenge.

*May 13th Happy Wedding Anniversary!*
It was the kind of morning when you feel like crawling down into the sleeping bag and staying there. Thanks to our optimus stove we had two coffees while still in bed — an unbeatable treat after the heavy rationing of our last month, but a strange way to celebrate our first anniversary.

We decided to lay over for the day. If the sun appeared later, we'd hike up into the mountains for a picnic lunch, but in the meantime we'd raise a tarp over the firepit and settle in.

Our anniversary day was in keeping with the style of our first year of marriage — simple, and spent in the heart of the northern mountains where life's real treasures lay. We stayed curled up by the fire, talking of the value of being alone for such an extended honeymoon. We now share a love for the north and a desire to spend many more anniversaries like this one.

*May 14th*
The morning was frightfully cold. I peeked out the tent to see a fresh cover of snow on the mountains, ice in the water bucket, and a frosty sheath on everything metal, then thought twice about rising before the sun. But to stay in bed would be to miss out on the best part of the day — sunrise and the chance to see game, so, with John on my heels, I dutifully emerged from the tent, muttering incoherently about the drawbacks of spring camping.

Soon the fire was sending up enough heat to warm us as we downed the morning eye opener. Only then did life seem worth living again, the pain of getting up and getting dressed in the frosty air behind us for another day.

We were slipping down the current by eight o'clock, just in time to watch the sun creep over the horizon's mountains.

For the next hour we stayed absolutely still, not even allowing our paddles to break the surface. The current carried us along while we looked for wildlife. Four Canada geese, honking and strutting on the north shore, spied us and took flight, and several moose eyed us from the wooded banks in their odd, almost perplexed way.

A dark round beast that looked like a bear cub lumbered into view. A second look confirmed wolverine — the characteristic blonde streak running along the side of its dark fur. Its peculiar gait was a sort of wavy motion in which front and then hindquarters rose and fell with each step as though all its sockets were loose. The animals apparently had not caught our scent and while we had it off guard, I took several pictures.

Not twenty minutes later I was framing another elusive creature in the viewfinder of the camera — a lone wolf, medium sized with a shiny coat of grey-black fur, timidly watching us as we passed.

We were back on course and floating down a slipwater when John looked back into a snye and saw a small porcupine in a clearing. An eddy conveniently turned up, so we were able to work our way back for pictures of him feeding on shoots.

Nothing is more exciting than capturing even brief glimpse of animals in their natural habitat. Our good fortune at such sightings made me more aware of the need to "travel clean" — leave no marks of human visitation in the backyards of these wild creatures.

In the early afternoon we landed on a gravel bar, less than a mile above where Brintnell Creek flows into the South Nahanni, intending to spend four days hiking. To the west is the country we want to see, the popular Glacier Lake, where the highest peaks of the Ragged Range — indeed the whole Northwest Territories — rise to more than nine thousand feet.

*May 18th*
Midday found us struggling through a dense stand of sprawling, snarled alder, with miserably heavy packs on and no notion of where the path was that had led us into Glacier Lake. Yesterday's rugged but exhilarating climb to the cirque (a natural amphitheatre surrounded by steep cliffs) at the base of Mount Harrison Smith was being overshadowed by our gruelling hike back to the South Nahanni.

A series of mishaps began soon after we left our base camp at the western end of Glacier Lake. On our hike in, the maps we needed for river travel fell from John's pack. We discovered their loss when we made our first camp, but instead of backtracking immediately to pick them up, we decided to recover them on our way out.

We were certain the maps had fallen out along the shoreline of the lake; so we kept our eyes peeled along the muddy bank. It was only after John doubled back over this first mile-long stretch that the maps turned up and we could continue on.

From the eastern end of the lake the trail weaves through forest, with fast flowing Brintnell Creek within earshot. About a mile along the trail is a second, smaller lake. While walking along its shoreline I dropped my gloves, but I had gone another half mile before realizing it. While I re-

*Mount Harrison Smith*

traced my steps, John prepared some hot soup. We downed a cup along with bannock and raisins before setting off again on the portage trail.

Within fifteen minutes we lost the trail blazes. Since the trail was well used and there appeared, on the way in, to be more than one path, we thought we could find our way out by simply following the clearest path through the mat of growth. We were wrong. Snow and fallen timber made it difficult to distinguish the path we sought from game trails and doubly tiresome to trudge over. Before long we knew we had erred, but we were too disoriented to turn back.

I was tired and cranky from hauling too-heavy a load over the trail and to complicate matters I was coming down with stomach cramps.

Even John's reserve of good spirits was beginning to wear down. He wore a grim expression that hinted he was frustrated too.

I tried to keep just enough distance between us so I wouldn't get slapped in the face when the foliaged ends of the alder sprang upright after he pushed his way through them, but I was beginning to lag behind.

Before long the gap between us lengthened and I found myself alone, surrounded by a tight mess of alder brush. I could still hear the snap and crunch of undergrowth as John bashed his way forward, but losing sight of him made me irritable. My face and hands were badly scratched and bleeding and my pack was continually getting caught up in branches. The cramps continued in waves of sharp pain that made me feel dizzy and weak.

"Jo, where are you?"

"Over here," I called back, but I was thoroughly fed up and didn't make much effort to be heard.

"Hey," came the reply, "I'll stay where I am. You follow my voice, okay?"

"Okay, okay," I grumbled, not loud enough for John to hear. Then realizing how foolish it was to have him worry, I screamed back some garbled message that made me sound like a wounded animal.

We met up, much to John's relief, as it was obvious from the look of me that I was not well. My choked and frustrated answer to whether or not I wanted to rest was an angry, "If I met up with a bear right now I'd tell him to get the blazes out of my way." John guided me to a log, removed my pack, and stuffed chocolate in my mouth.

What I really needed was a few minutes to get hold of myself. Regardless of how ill I felt, we had to keep moving. Finding the portage trail was a hopeless dream, so we would just have to continue bushwacking until we reached the river. We had seen from a height of land the direction it lay in.

As we pushed on I had recurrent memories of a film I had seen about a long distance runner overcoming the psychological and physiological wall at twenty miles of a marathon and pushing the final six miles to win the race. I wasn't quite sure if I had passed or was approaching such a wall myself, but as long as my legs continued to support me I was still in the race, I figured.

By seven o'clock we were back in camp, itching from mosquito bites, sore and tired. But we were home and that was all that really mattered.

We were half a day's paddle from the western boundry of Nahanni National Park and Rabbitkettle Lake, where we planned to spend a few days. There was a PanAbode (prefabricated cabin) set up on the lakeshore a short portage away from the river — an unoccupied warden station that would be our stopover while we took in the area's sights. The most notable of these was reported to be Rabbitkettle Hotsprings, two mounds of coral-like tufa formed from the precipitation of calcium carbonate. Water rises out of the springs year-round at twenty-one degrees Celsius. The largest formation rises to a height of ninety feet and is over two hundred feet in diameter.

Being within the park meant that for the remainder of our journey we would be in contact with Lou, the chief park warden, via two way radio. All visitors check in at stations along the river, but since we were travelling before the official park opening date a different system had to be worked out to monitor our progress. Lou had kindly offered to let us stay overnight at the cabins and use the radio to phone in our progress reports.

My ill health could not have been more aptly timed. With the beautiful surroundings of Rabbitkettle Lake to take in from my bedside, my recovery was sure to be hastened. Nowhere else have I seen such a peaceful atmosphere. The peaks of Glacier Lake that dominate the horizon to the northwest, the mountain pass of Hole-in-the-Wall River to the southeast and the rounded mountains to the south, bordering the Flat and Rabbitkettle rivers are a snowy backdrop for a jewel of a lake. The use of the warden's cabin is the icing on the cake.

*May 22nd*
How easy it is to sink back into the comforts of more civilized living.

The variety of culinary gadgets makes me feel like a poor waif who had never seen a well-equipped kitchen before. There is even a gas stove and a stainless steel sink, fancy dishes, and soft vinyl chairs around the kitchen table. The only thing missing is a cotton dress and sandals. My year-old army pants with patches over the patches and one of John's old faded shirts don't quite make the grade in these spic and span surroundings.

The animals in the area make our paddles around the lake a sheer delight. This evening we watched, undetected, as a black bear roamed the shoreline beaches, his rolls of fat jiggling as he lumbered along.

The streamlined heads of two otters broke the stillness of the water as they swam in circles in the shallows. Their closeness to the dock in front of the cabin diverted us from the bear's clownish behaviour. We didn't move a muscle as we watched, noticing for the first time the humming-birds flitting above the branches on the lakeshore. When several minutes passed without the otters making a move we continued our paddle.

In the middle of the lake, we squeezed one end of our fishing rods between our legs and supported the other end on the gunwale of the canoe so we could take turns on the paddle and behind the eye of the camera. Back and forth across the lake we floated, as silently as a warship lurking in enemy waters, until we were practically in the middle of a flock of more than a hundred ducks. Suddenly, they took flight and we sat in silence, listening to the medley of caws, honks and quacks, made even more dramatic by the wild flapping of wings and splash of webbed feet kicking out of the water. The birds circled once over our heads, still squawking frantically and then alighted on the calm surface of the lake again just a few yards from where they had taken off. When darkness approached we headed for shore.

*May 23rd*

An end must come to all things and we felt we had outstayed the park staff's hospitable offer. It was with great regret (an entire summer was more my idea of a suitable length of stay at Rabbitkettle Lake) that we packed up soon after breakfast and portaged our gear back to the river.

We learned on our arrival at the Butte that John's well meaning farewell gesture — restocking the woodbox — was the one slip-up of our stay at the cabin. He quite innocently cut up four poles that were lying on the ground next to the cabin, only to learn that these had been intended for the building of a new cache.

We were only twenty minutes on the water before we began spotting game. We made what was now a well-rehearsed approach towards a wolverine — the best-groomed and most nourished looking animal we had

*The gawking moose*

*Bald eagle*

set eyes on. His sleek and shiny coat of fur was indication of how bountiful the land was.

Farther on we saw three moose (all cows), more flocks of ducks (mallards and American widgeons) Canada geese, a pair of playful otters sliding down a mud bank, beavers skimming the surface of the snyes — all reminders that the park was a wildlife sanctuary.

During our three day layover, the water has risen considerably. This we were glad to see, because the next seventy-five miles is said to be a slacker South Nahanni. We hope an increase in volume will have some effect on the speed of the current and help our daily mileage. Not until we enter the canyons beyond Virginia Falls (the next landmark on the river will we see any major rapids.

The landscape is changing. The mountains are more rounded, with straight walls and the valley itself much broader — in contrast to the craggy peaks we saw during the first sixty miles.

### May 26th

This morning, while passing a large island, we saw a moose in the alder bushes. Immediately we aligned the canoe so we could drift closer. Although we had seen plenty of moose over the year (and collected enough bones of the dead variety to put together a full skeleton) we were anxious to find out more about this particular animal. This was the time of the year when the cows gave birth to their calves and sought protection against predators by staying on the islands. We hoped we had chanced upon a mother and her calf.

We were disappointed when our would-be cow moose turned out to be a young bull, but I clicked off three pictures quickly, thinking he would stride off at any moment. This animal, however, was evidently not briefed on the protocol of meeting humans. He did not turn and run, but rather stood and gawked at us as we floated up to him, tipped our hats and waved at him, then floated away. Moose have been accused of being dull by nature, but this fellow was carrying things a bit far. What was the matter with him we wondered. Was he dumbfounded? Inquisitive? Half asleep? Paralyzed? Dead?

Later, we met up with more valley residents — porcupine, herring gulls, a sandpiper, mallards, geese, and beavers. But by far the most memorable moment was when we slipped around a slow bend in the river and spotted two bald eagles, a male and a female, soaring over the water searching for dead fish.

We expected the birds to disappear, until we saw their nest, high up in a dead poplar. That decided our course of action. We unpacked tripod and extender and made ready to stand our vigil — all night if we had to — to capture a still shot of them landing.

The loud flapping of their powerful wings and their menacing "caws" as they circled above our heads were frightening, so we took turns behind the camera while the other flailed a paddle about in a feeble act of self-defence. Fortunately, they decided to keep their distance.

Watching these birds fly is to witness a beautiful sight. The huge wings are fully extended, the white tail feathers spread out in a fan. The white head is held forward and slightly down, the yellow beak plainly visible, with its cruel hook-like tip.

We watched as the pair lifted off and landed on wavering spruce tops, dove like fighter bombers at the water one minute and soared on the wind the next. We stilled the action shot we wanted, but only a movie projector could have done justice to these birds' graceful flight.

*May 27th*

The majesty of Virginia Falls is beyond imagining. They are twice the height of Niagara Falls — almost three hundred feet — and their wild mountainuous setting enhances them further. Their thunderous roar from a distance instils all the nervousness and excitement that precedes a great event.

We paddled the last mile of placid water above the falls, trying to imagine what the explorers felt when they first discovered this breathtaking waterfall. Albert Faille, a legendary character of these parts, whose portage trail around the falls is still in use today, must have been awestruck — better still, thunderstruck, when he first saw the wall of falling water.

We followed the one-mile portage to the foot of the falls for our first look, thinking that a close up from below would offer the best effect. It did. The calamitous roar of the thundering water left me dizzy. The sun's rays reflecting off the rising clouds of mist, the iridescent effect of the jets of spray, the yellow foaming river that crashed against the the rocks and churned in the pool at the base of the giant curtain were sensational.

Three-quarters of the way back up the portage boardwalk is a blazed trail that leads out onto a point above the falls. From the edge of the point we could see the river split around the austere rock pinnacle that towers above and in the midst of the tumbling water. This section of whitewater (appropriately referred to as the Sluice Box) is as violent as the falls themselves. The volume of water is enough to scare the wits out of you, let alone the speed at which it moves.

We spent the rest of the afternoon crouched on the rim of a ledge at waterlevel, totally mesmerized. At our feet was a seething cauldron of

*Virginia Falls*

waves and foam — a watershed that drops swiftly over a series of steep ledges before plunging straight off the brink if it rushes right or spiralling around the rock column if it skirts left.

*May 28th*

We could not have asked for a more perfect day for our hike up Sunblood Mountain. Not a cloud showed against the blue sky and just a slight wind was blowing. When our belongings were safely cached we filled our day packs and canoed across the river.

The wind carried the soft fragrance of the mountain avens, lady's slipper, buttercups, and wild roses, all blooming in the woods at the base of the mountain. It was the first time we'd seen so many wild flowers. We noticed, too, how much more fertile the soil appeared and wondered if the river had once covered this area of land.

At the foot of Sunblood, we stared up at the rock slide that fanned down the mountain side. It would be our climbing route.

"Three hours should see us at the top." John said as he led the way.

And three hours later we were resting on a grass covered meadow. We sat on the mountain top with a full and striking view of Virginia Falls and the deep canyon walls downriver, where the Nahanni flowed in curves through folds of the Mackenzie Mountains.

The next stage of our trip would take us through this unglaciated section of the river where the valley's legends had originated. From the falls to Nahanni Butte we could stop on every sandbar and ask ourselves, Was this once a campsite of Patterson's or Faille's?

*May 29th*

It was too brisk a morning to want to do anything but get on the move, which was just as well, for we each had two more loads to carry over the portage trail that bypassed the falls — we had carried one load the night before. As portages go, the one mile hike was not difficult. Climbing back up the steepest section was the hardest part, especially as our legs are still spongy from yesterday's climb.

Following a scrupulous check to ensure that every article we carried was tied into the canoe and the spray cover properly fitted, we pored over the maps for the last time and took a long serious look at the first bend of Five Mile Gorge.

Ahead of us was a section of the South Nahanni River that was sure to be a test, especially for me, because I was a novice whitewater canoeist. But my lack of experience in rapids didn't bother me. I knew what was

*Pulpit Rock*

expected of me as bowsman and I felt confident. I would listen carefully to everything John said to me, for in our canoe he was the expert.

To help me develop an eye for reading whitewater more skilfully, we made it a practice at the head of each set of rapids for me to describe to John what conditions I saw and what route I thought was the best for us to take. He listened closely while I talked of the obstacles around the opening bend of the Gorge.

"We'll have to stay left. Those standing waves on the right — we'll find ourselves washed into the wall if we get too near them. When going left we'll have to avoid those two rocks." I pointed out the two I meant. "Looks as though we go left on the first and to the right on the second."

"OK, good, Jo," came the prompt and positive reply, "But watch for hidden rocks."

Almost as soon as we shoved off we were into high standing waves and a current so swift it was nearly impossible to stop. But we were riding the high rollers so suddenly I had no time to get jittery.

The waves came crashing over the bow as we guided the canoe around the first bend, John bellowing at me to keep paddling hard after we manoeuvred past the first two rocks. Then we sped around the second bend and saw for the first time what lay ahead.

"Oh, my God!" John exclaimed.

I was so frightened I nearly dropped my paddle. If an experienced whitewater canoeist like John was awestruck, small wonder that I was downright terrified.

"I don't need to hear that!" I hollered back, but there wasn't time for John to answer.

The canoe felt as though it were suspended on the crest of a wave.

"Paddle hard through this stuff, Jo"

Water exploded over the bow and I was drenched when the canoe finally slid down the wave.

Then, as suddenly, we were jerked by the violent thrust of more waves — these ones shallow and more irregular. All I remember is the sensation of moving so swiftly that reference points along the shore were just a blur. I kept my eyes riveted on the water directly in front, paddling hard on every stroke, trying to dig the paddle blade into the fury of water. Taking a canoe out on a turbulent sea could not have been more hair-raising.

We made it through all five miles of the wild water and took a break at Marengo Creek to stop my heart from pounding in my throat. I was tight in the shoulders and the arms, probably more from tension than exertion. It wasn't long before I regained my composure and was ready to get back into the canoe. John laughed uproariously when he saw me rummage through my pack for fieldglasses, because he knew I wanted to see what the Gorge looked like from below. He accused me of developing an ardent passion for large waves when I mentioned going back and trying the run again."

You've joined the ranks, Jo," he added fondly. "The sign of a white-water nut is wanting to go back and try it again."

The sun was directly overhead when we reached the portage trail that bypasses the Rapid-That-Runs-Both-Ways. A black bear was wandering along the edge of the forest, but he seemed more than happy to yield and give us the right of way on the trail. With camera and gun in hand, we hiked to the moss-covered point where we could scout the rapids.

The river makes a great right turn just above the rapids, but cannot manage the left immediately after. The water shoots for the point of land on which we were standing and splits in two. Half of the rush of water circles clockwise in an upper bay (where our canoe sat), and the other half rages downstream.

The upper bay is congested with floating debris but it is calm compared with its sister below. The lower eddy is a boiling torrent.

John studied the rapids for a minute, then said we could make a flawless run. I gulped. This was the worst rapid on the river — the only place other than Virginia Falls that had a portage route around it. We had agreed to see it before deciding, but I should have known what John would say. He had often referred to this rapid as the greatest challenge, and now he considered it to be within our capability.

I listened silently while he explained his strategy. I knew I was being railroaded, but John's enthusiasm and confidence were so great, that I began to believe we could do it, although one look at the maelstrom below told me I was crazy. He knew I'd say yes, but he'd just have to wait till I was ready.

On our way back to the canoe John coached me to keep my centre of gravity low. "Balance is the key," he said, as much to himself as to me, as we loaded ourselves into the canoe above the rapid and upstream ferried into the main current.

What had looked like fairly placid water above the rapids was in fact a seething mass of irresistible suction. The canoe was picking up speed, rising and falling on the rollers. We were beyond turning back.

We had rehearsed the critical moment before beginning the run and when daylight suddenly appeared to my left, I knew my moment of glory had arrived. A good draw stroke was needed to pull us into the calmer water. My arms were already in motion when John yelled out the single command.

But something was wrong! My draw should have acted as a pivot, but nothing seemed to be grabbing the paddle. It might as well have been in mid-air. I dug deeper and held my breath.

My reference points were changing. One minute I was looking downstream, the next I was facing the jagged wall of black rock. John must have been swinging the stern around.

"Paddle, Jo! Paddle!"

Suddenly the canoe shot into calm water. We had missed the eddy by only a few inches.

An hour later we were at the intersection of the Flat and South Nahanni rivers. From there we tracked the canoe past the sandbars and shallow rock beaches to the warden's station on the Flat River.

Once the first of the season's mosquitoes were flushed out of the cabin and Bic coils lit to keep them at bay, we settled into an evening of washing hair, bodies, and clothes — anything to feel human again. It was a great shock, as it had been at Rabbitkettle Lake, to peer into a mirror and see what looked back at me. What had once been a face spotted with freckles had, over the days, turned into a leathery piece of hide. There wasn't a sprinkling of freckles any longer either — I looked evenly tanned. Even more noticeable was the lack of flesh on my cheeks.

*May 31st*

I woke with a start. The only part of me not bundled up was my nose, and it was so cold, I couldn't sleep another wink.

I shuffled across the cold floor in a groggy stupor to light the stove — an antique that stood next to the door. I stuffed crumpled paper and wood shavings into the woodbox and lit a match under the pile. Almost instantly smoke began to drift out of the stove's seams.

I tinkered with every knob and gadget sticking out of the thing, but couldn't open the vent. Clouds of smoke were beginning to fill the cabin, while I sputtered and choked, without a clue as to what to do.

The dense smoke woke John and forced him out of the top bunk. We could barely see through the heavy pall, let alone breathe. I flung the door open and staggered outside, barefoot and in my nightie. John was close behind.

When I looked at John — still half-awake — and then at the cabin, I doubled over in laughter.

Smoke was pouring out of every opening — the front door, the window seams, the spaces between the wall logs — everywhere.

"I trust we aren't burning this thing to the ground, Joanne."

The cabin did indeed look like a smokestack ready to explode.

"Stay here," John said. "I'll open the draft." He was inside again before I could explain myself. In no time the stack was drawing smoke and John was back outside. He was now awake.

By evening we were camped fifty miles from Flat River with a view of the Funeral Range and recollections of the sights we had seen through the Third Canyon — especially Pulpit Rock. At the Gate, midway through the Third Canyon, the river makes a ninety degree turn. Pulpit Rock, a pinnacle shaped as its name suggests, is a distinctive landmark on the eastern bank.

We had fought a head wind most of the day, along with weather so changeable we had worn four different sets of clothing to cover us during the downpours, light drizzles, high winds and sunshine. We had seen the impressive canyon in every light.

Its sheer-walled cliffs, rise seven hundred feet above the river, creating an open-tunnel effect and making the current seem even faster than it is. We stopped at sandbars to photograph the cliffs, preferring not to stand in the canoe or divert our attention from the rolling waves on the river.

Downstream from our campsite, in the shadow of early darkness (it was eleven o'clock), loomed the bare faces of the Headless Range and the opening to Second Canyon. Tomorrow we will travel through it into Deadmen Valley — the stomping grounds of Patterson and his partner, Gordon Matthews, fifty years ago.

*June 1st*

When not in the shade of the east canyon walls, the sun beat directly down on us and we shed some of our heavy clothing. There was no wind here, so we could drift along as carefree as we pleased, studying every cleft in the precipitous cliff faces through the binoculars. We were on the lookout for Dall sheep.

John's driving motive, on every mountain ledge he teetered on and for every tedious hour he spent with fieldglasses glued to his face — during even the most foul weather — was to spot these white mountain sheep. Up to now we had not seen one. A good number of white rock faces had looked like sheep, mind you, but they were never the real McCoy. We had

*Deadmen Valley*

been told the canyons offered the best chance of a sighting, but our trip thus far was a failure if judged by the number of Dall sheep framed in the lens of our camera.

I knew my spouse too well to think we wouldn't be scaling more than our fair share of cliffs before the day ended. How close to one of these "cliff hangers" would we have to get before John was perfectly happy? As this was his ultimate dream, I knew a distant sighting wouldn't satisfy him.

I was pessimistic about sighting these rare creatures, because we were not planning a hike into the heart of the mountains where I thought the herds grazed, chewed their cuds, frolicked on rock spires and did whatever else sheep do to occupy their time. The rising level of the South Nahanni made such a side trip impractical. We had promised ourselves we would stay clear of the river in flood, and every day that passed brought us closer to danger. John was even more adamant than I about this, but he also believed we deserved to see sheep. Therefore we would.

His faith and perserverance were rewarded. Five hundred feet or so above us, on a narrow ledge, was a moving white object. It was the first authentic Dall sheep we had laid eyes on.

Once the canoe was safely beached on the sandbar of an island, my attention turned to the vertical face of the rock wall. While John focused on the majestic young ram, I was busy calculating, on a scale of one to ten, how utterly ridiculous it would be to try to approach the animal. Taking my obvious bias into account. I still came up with a nine. We were not properly equipped for climbing such a rock wall.

There was no need to fuss though; John agreed. He was perfectly happy to alternate between zoom lens and fieldglasses to follow the careful moves of the ram. It was making its way to the highest point of the cliff, balancing itself on ledges so narrow I felt sure it would tumble into the river. Once at the top, it disappeared, and we continued our paddle.

John was ebullient, but the quest was not over yet.

By noon we were approaching the end of the canyon without having captured the perfect shot, so John decided it was time to climb a cliff. I resigned myself to the inevitable as graciously as I could. The best bet seemed to be a cliff near Murder Creek, so named because it was here, in 1906, that the headless bodies of the McLeod brothers were discovered. A sheep trail wound its way up the side of the cliff and at the top followed the rim to a series of higher ledges. If so inclined, and John was, one could walk for miles along the very edge of this cliff. I was psyching myself up for just that when John frantically motioned me to keep low and be quiet. He had spied something on the next rise.

Sure enough it was a sheep, another ram, three or four years old we judged from the half curl of his horns, and asleep.

I stayed behind while John crawled up to the sheep. It was a safe enough climb and the wind was in John's favour, but I couldn't help thinking we were in one of the most mysterious spots in the valley — anything could happen here.

Staying close to the ground and trying to find cover in the sparse vegetation, John advanced slowly and quietly upward. Not quietly enough though. The sheep suddenly bounded up on all fours as if touched with a electric prod and hit the trail on the run.

John gave chase for a few yards but it was no contest. The sheep sprinted up the scree, heading for a stony crevice, and increased the distance between itself and John by a wider margin with each leap.

John had pictures that pleased him, but I was lucky enough to get a close-up view that I don't think I'll ever forget. Sitting where I was, on the highest tip of a knoll directly below where the sheep had been resting, I could watch its every move through the binoculars. I was so close that all I framed was its face, which had lines as chiselled as the rocks in which it lived and a chamois-smooth texture. But its most distinctive feature was its huge protruding eyes and heavy lids.

We remained on the ridge for lunch, surveying the splendid panorama of Deadmen Valley, a basin of colourful forests, its host of green highlighted by the grey mountains with the last of their winter snows. Through it all a silty Nahanni meandered around innumerable islands, gravel bars and newly formed driftpiles. Our stop for the night would be Sheaf Creek, where Patterson and Matthews had built their cabin in 1928 (it is no longer standing) and there was no doubt what the evening's entertainment would be — a reread of *The Dangerous River*, Patterson's own tale about the legendary valley.

### June 3rd

Two days of covering some of the ground Patterson called home in 1928-29 were behind us when we rounded the last turn into First Canyon. For John and me, standing on the beach that overlooked what Patterson called his "home eddy" was more than just a moment of stepping back in time to the year in a man's life we had so enjoyed reading about. We felt an association between Patterson and ourselves and could vividly picture his sheep-hunting expeditions on the Tlogotsho Plateau, the trails he covered when venturing out on cold winter days to the trapline and, most of all, his adventures on the river.

We studied the mountains that Patterson and Matthews had roamed, walked through the woods where their cabin once stood, and hiked along the banks of Dry Canyon and Prairie and Ram creeks, just as they had fifty years before.

No man's story can ever be shared absolutely by another, but many dreams can be born from hearing of another's accomplishments — as had happened to John and me. For us, only an entire summer spent exploring would do justice to the history of the area. The tentative itinerary was already being formulated in our minds.

We maintained an earnest sheep patrol through the last of the river's great canyons, but could not repeat our earlier good fortune. That, too, would have to wait for another time, for the South Nahanni was rising steadily. The heaviest downpours we had endured started soon after our arrival in Patterson's home territory and left us in a permanent state of dampness for two days.

Despite the acrid odour — that sinus-clearing smell of rotten eggs — surrounding the Kraus Hotsprings (Gus and Mary Kraus lived next to these sulphur springs for over thirty years), we made camp for the night. The luxury of a mineral bath was too exciting to pass up. We were some fifty miles from civilization — a day's paddle away. During our last evening on the shores of the South Nahanni we were content to sit by the campfire and listen to the water's low rumble and its lapping against the shore.

A year ago to the day we had arrived at Big Island Lake.

I couldn't believe the time was 3.15 a.m. or that John was huddled around the fire, flipping pancakes and scambling eggs in such disgusting weather. The rain was smacking against the tent walls and overhead tarp but, undaunted, John had risen to prepare a breakfast-in-the-sleeping-bags celebration.

"This is the big day, Joey."

"John! It's three in the morning!"

"Three-fifteen — time to get up. Get on the water early, you know."

I slumped back into the tent, hoping to wake up a second time and discover it was all a miserable dream.

I was roused a second time, with a plateful of food that I decided to accept in the same good spirit in which it was offered. What was the point of resisting?

Half-past five and we were off, headed for the Butte. We were entering thirty miles of river called The Splits — a multi-channeled Nahanni where the hazards are not eddies and riffles but a mess of driftpiles, sweepers, deadheads, and sandbars you don't see until you've run aground. We paddled steadily through the rain for eight hours. To stop would have been even more miserable.

When my arms began to get sore I conjured up a mental image of a large leafy green salad with blue cheese dressing, and slabs of bread and butter on my plate.

When we stopped for lunch we were about fifteen miles from the Butte. The sun had finally appeared, so we dried a few things out by the fire while enjoying hot tea, bannock, and the last tin of liver paté.

Only when we set off on the final leg of our journey did it hit me — apprehension about returning east and what the world outside would be like after a year of solitude. We had lived day in and day out engulfed in blissful peace, sometimes deeply affected by the tranquility and loveliness of the natural world, other times not mindful of how fortunate we were.

Ten miles away was the Indian village of Nahanni Butte and on the nub of land a short paddle downstream, the warden station — civilization for John and me. We heard the sound of an engine in the distance. Thinking it might be a helicopter flying low, we searched the sky. It was not the burr and whip of a helicopter though, it was an outboard motor — Lou and four others, travelling upstream towards us in a jet boat.

Nahanni Trailhead was over.

# Epilogue

John and I spent seven days as guests of the Nahanni National Park staff, during which time we were reintroduced to the amenities of civilization without the hustle and bustle of a crowd. We were thankful for this opportunity to adjust to such things as radios, soft mattresses, running water, different foods and new faces.

Once on the move, first by aircraft to Fort Nelson, British Columbia, and then by speeding taxi to a hotel in the centre of town, it was all we could do to hang onto our sense of humour. A strange feeling that we were from another planet began to surface.

In the first few days, slabs of concrete, automation, loud noises, crowds and the sense that everything and everyone around us was in constant, harried motion repulsed us. Feeling disoriented and sad that we might not see our cabin again for months, even years, we wondered aloud why we had left the wilderness.

We had lived a peaceful existence, rich in the way that making it on your own can be. We had lived with the bare essentials of food, clothing and shelter and we had lived contented with that simplicity. It was going to take time before we felt the need for and could fully accept the luxuries of civilization. What we really wanted to do was return to the mountains and forests and find overselves again.

A gradual acclimatization to our new surroundings did take place. When we reached Watson Lake, Yukon, and our trusty Volvo (it had survived a year set on blocks), we tidied up our affairs and then pointed ourselves eastward. Each day that passed found us more accepting of daily city living. Soon we were not offended by the cost of restaurant food or the price of gasoline and thoughts of reunions with our families heightened our spirits.

Slideshows and the writing of this book have kept the memories of our homesteading venture alive — a promise we made to ourselves the day we left the cabin. I quite expect that detailed recollections and frequent flashbacks of a most wonderful, valuable year will become hazy, but one thing for certain will not. Tucked away in the backs of our consciousness is a deep love for the northern wilderness and an everlasting regard for the self-awareness and self-sufficiency it taught us.

*Appendix*

# The Black Book

*Building Materials*

| | |
|---|---|
| Door bolts | 16 heavy screw bolts |
| Door hinges and screws | 2 heavy duty hinges and screws |
| Door lock | 1 inside/outside latch |
| Window panes | 8 sheets of plexiglass |
| Window sills | 2″ × 10″ Spruce — 16 pieces — slotted |
| Door/Window sealant | 6 tubes — 1 heat resistant for stovepipe |
| Tarpaper | 420 square feet for roof cover |
| Nails — 2″ flathead | 300 — to nail down tarpaper |
| — 4″ common | 1470 — general construction |
| — 6″ common | 100 — stress areas |
| Sheet metal screws | 30 — hold pipes, elbows and cover secure |
| Plywood | 9 pieces — one for table top |

*Building Equipment*

| | |
|---|---|
| Caulking gun | 1 |
| Chain saw #1 | small, detail work |
| Chain saw #2 | large, powerful |
| Repair: | |
|   Spare chains | 2 for 16″ bar |
|   Tune-up wrenches | 2 — 1 for each |
|   Grease gun | for lubricating powertips |
|   Filters | 2 gas, 1 air filter per machine |
|   Rivets | for chain repair |
|   Starter cord | 4 feet |
| Gasoline | regular — 3 5-gallon jugs |
| Chain oil — medium | 1 gallon |
| — light | 1 quart for winter sawing |
| Strainer/Funnel | 1 — no-splash cover |
| Grease for gun | 1 tube for grease gun |
| Crazy glue | 1 tube |
| Adz | squaring and levelling |
| Axes | 3 — lighweight; 1 — splitter |
| File — heavy | square, large — sharpen adz and axes |

218

| | |
|---|---|
| Files — light | round — for chainsaws; triangular for utility |
| Whetstone | small — final sharpening |
| Finishing hammer | 1 |
| Shovel | 1 normal workhorse |
| Plane | 1 large — for furniture building |
| Surform | 1 regular size — fine smoothing |
| Surform spare blade | 1 — to fit surform |
| Level | 18″ aluminum |
| Chalk line | 25′ — squaring/halving timbers |
| Chalk refill | 1 small tube |
| Tape measure | roll up type — 50′ |
| String | 1 large spool for squaring cabin |
| Tarp | large poly — pre-cabin storage |
| Brace and bit drill | furniture, repair Grumman |
| Wood drill bits | 3 — ½″, 1″, 1½″ |
| Scribers | notch cutting |
| Lumber crayon | 1 large red for notching |
| Chisels | 2 — ¾″ and 1¼″ |
| Square | 1′ steel square |
| C-clamps | 2 for repair work — 2½″ opening |
| Eye level | general grade work |
| Small swede saw | 1 lightweight |
| Spare blade for swede saw | 1 — taped to backboard |
| Carpenter's apron | 2 |
| Hard hat | 2 — 1 faceguard attachment |
| Hand cleaner | small jar — clean grease and spruce gum |
| Block and tackle | 4:1 ratio for heavy lifting |
| Rope | 400′ of poly rope — yellow — general use |
| Wire | 1 roll — repair, joints, construction |
| Log peeler | Marples drawknife |
| Log splitter wedge | 1 lightweight |
| Spare axe handle | 1 |
| Saw | normal for woodworking, furniture |
| Propane torch kit | 1 container propane, heads, lighter |

*House*

| | |
|---|---|
| Stove | stepstove to heat 315 square feet |
| Stove bricks | 100 lbs — fragile |
| Stove pipes | 3 normal — 1 insulated for roof |
| Stove pipe elbows | 3 |
| Accessories: | |
|   flashings | 2 |
|   insulated pipe hangers | 1 pair |
|   rain cap | 1 |

| | |
|---|---|
| Lanterns | Coleman — 1 large and 1 small |
| Mantles and generator | spares for lanterns |
| Lantern fuel | 4 5-gallon jugs — 1 jug for backpacking stove |
| Candles | fifty |
| Disposable flashlights | six for use in tent in winter |
| Matches | 50 boxes — one case |
| Waterproof matches | 4 BIC Lighters |
| Mirror | 4 plates — personal admiration society |
| Broom | 1 regular |
| Teatowels | 3 regular |
| Toilet seat | 1 regular |
| Two-Way radio | Spilsbury SSB |
| Radio batteries | 2 spare sets of alkaline |
| Radio aerials | 2 Spilsbury and one heavy duty |
| Canadian flag | 1 — patriotism |
| Gun | .303 Lee-Enfield |
| Ammunition | 40 boxes — straight grain centre fire |
| Gun-Cleaning case | swabs, nitro, oil and rod |
| Tool Box: | |
|   Multi-screwdriver | 1 — tips to fit equipment needs |
|   Nut loosener | 1 jar — for the impossible ones |
|   Vice-grips | 1 large pair |
|   Pliers | large — for general and wire work |
|   3-In-One oil | general oiling |
|   Adjustable wrench | 1 large, for repairs |
| Washing tub | large tub for washing and general |
| Washboard | 2′ × 3′ — cleaning clothes |
| Sink | plastic sink with drain and plug |
| Sink hose | 4′ — for kitchen |
| Thermometers | 2 — one indoor, one outdoor |
| Foam pad for bed | 1 large pad |
| Pillow cases | 2 — stuff with out-of-season clothes |
| Sleeping bags | 4 — 2 polarguard, 2 down |
| Awl/Waxed thread | 1 |
| Awl accessories | spare needles and roll of waxed thread |
| Fire extinguisher | 1 for emergency |
| Clothespins | 40 |
| Oven mitts | 1 pair |
| Water carrier | 1 plastic collapsible, one gallon |

*First Aid*

| | |
|---|---|
| Vitamin C | 100 tablets for the winter |
| Halazon tablets | 25 — water purifier |

| | |
|---|---|
| Butterfly swabs | 100 sterilized cleaning |
| Q-Tips | 400 |
| Cotton balls | 1 pack |
| Thermometer | 1 internal — record body temperature |
| Gauze | 4 rolls |
| Steri-Strips | 2 packages — major pain relief |
| Adhesive tape | 4 rolls |
| 222 tablets | 2 jars — mild pain relief |
| Insect bite kit | loaded needle |
| Toothache drops | 1 jar Jiffy |
| Kaopectate | 1 500ml jar |
| Elastoplast | 3 boxes |
| Tensor bandages | 2 — 1 small and 1 large |
| Ozonal | 2 tubes |
| Contac-C | 1 package — colds |
| Neo-Citran | 24 packages — colds |
| Anacin | 2 small packages — headaches |
| Nail clippers | 1 large, 2 regular |
| Scissors | 2 pair — one regular, one collapsible |
| Lypsol | 3 tubes — lip protection |
| Hand lotion | 4 bottles of Intensive Care |
| Extra glasses | 1 prescription pair for John |
| 292 | 1 prescription — serious pain |
| Demerol | 1 prescription — serious illness/pain |
| Calamine lotion | 1 jar — mosquito bites |
| Anivy | 1 tube for poison ivy/skin rash |
| Infarub | 1 large tube — muscle pain |
| Safety pins | 30 — assorted sizes |
| Needles | 30 assorted sizes — slivers, repairs |
| Thread | One spool — emergency |
| First aid book | Red Cross Manual |
| Throat lozenges | 3 packages |
| Exlax | 1 package |
| Antibiotics | 1 presciption |
| Moleskin | 2 large rolls for blisters |

*Transportation*

| | |
|---|---|
| Canoe | Grumman — 18-foot aluminum |
| Duct tape | 2 rolls for rapid repairs |
| Liquid aluminum | 1 tube for more permanent repairs |
| Neoprene rubber | 1 square foot for permanent repairs |
| Rivets | 1 bag of 50 |
| Aluminum sheet | 2 square feet |
| Small drill bit | 1 for drilling rivet holes — fit wood drill |

| | |
|---|---|
| Rope | 2 50-feet painters |
| Volvo | 144S — 1969 — 110,000 miles |
| Trailer hitch for Volvo | 1 installed — heavy duty |
| Repair kit: | |
|   Headlights guards | Chicken wire over entire front end |
|   Spare tire | 1 |
|   Fan belt, fuses, oil | |
|   Brake/Clutch fluid | 1 of each |
| Oil water and gas | Use jugs for chainsaw gas |
| Car topper | carry canoe on top of Volvo |
| Paddles | 2 aluminum, 2 wood |
| Life preservers | 2 ensolite body jackets |
| Bailers | 2 carved out javex jugs |
| Maps | 1:250,000 covered in clear Mac-Tac |
| Aerial Photos | 2 photos of Island Lakes region |
| Nylon backpacks | 2 Camptrails |
| Canvas canoe packs | 2 packs — one with axe pouch |
| Spray cover | Grumman — with steel cable tightener |

*Clothing*

| | |
|---|---|
| Hats | 2 — protection from the sun |
| Toques | 2 — keep head warm |
| Scarfs | 2 Wigwam neck protectors and 1 wool |
| Work Gloves | 4 pair |
| Mitts | 4 pair |
| Cold Weather Gloves | 2 pair — down mitts with wool backings |
| 60/40 rain parkas | 2 |
| Down vests | 2 |
| Cold weather parka | 2 — double parkas good to -60°C |
| Light work pants | 4 pair — dry easily — army green |
| Cold weather pants | 2 — down with side zippers |
| Wool sox | 50 pair of Wigwam Sox |
| Down sox | 2 pair |
| Work boots | 2 pair of light hiking boots |
| Normal underwear | 4 pair per person |
| Thermal underwear | 2 sets per person |
| Wool pants | 2 pair — for medium cold days |
| Shorts | 2 pair — hot days, swimming, dreaming |
| Turtlenecks/T-Shirts | 8 pair — general use |
| Sweaters | 6 sweaters — all wool |
| Face protector | 2 down guards for extreme cold conditions |
| Ski goggles | 2 — eye/sun glare protection |
| Rain poncho | 2 nylon ponchos with pockets |
| Rain chaps | 2 pair |

| | |
|---|---|
| Gaiters | 2 pair — skiing and spring hiking |
| In-cabin pants | 4 pair — special-occasion and general jean and cords |
| | |
| Towels | 4 regular |
| Face cloth | 2 regular |
| Toothbrushs | 3 regular |
| Dental floss | 4 rolls |
| Nail brush | 1 regular for cleaning |
| Hair brush/comb | 2 combination (Avon) and one brush |
| Razor and blades | 1 razor and 50 blades |
| Shaving foam | 8 cans |
| Handkerchiefs | 4 cotton |
| Sewing kit | needles, buttons, thread, Velcro |
| Contact solution | for Joanne contact lenses |
| Down booties | 2 pair with cordura bottoms |
| Knickers | 2 pair — skiing and spring hiking |
| Down tie | John's — for special occasions when nothing less will do |

*Cooking / Eating*

| | |
|---|---|
| Coleman oven | for baking over stove and fire |
| Bread pans | 2 regular |
| Muffin tins | 2 6-muffin tins |
| Cake pans | 1 8″ |
| Pie shells | 1 12″ |
| Large pot | 1 15-gallon pot with lid |
| Pots | set of 3 nesting pots |
| Strainer | 1 regular |
| Shaker | 1 regular |
| Fry pans | 2 — one heavy and one light |
| Tea pot | 1 regular |
| Dishes | set of 4 — Melmac |
| Utensils | set of 4 — knife, fork and spoon |
| Bulk item storage jars | 4 old coffee tins |
| Cooking Utensils: | |
|   Flipper | 2 regular |
|   Whisk | 1 regular |
|   Knives | 2 — one bread and one heavy duty |
|   Can opener | 2 — one regular and one survival |
|   Measuring Cups/spoons | 3 piece set — plastic |
|   Baster | 1 regular |

*Recreation*

| | |
|---|---|
| Camera | 1 Pentax MX, instructions, 50mm lens |

| | |
|---|---|
| Tripod | 1 lightweight — Slik |
| Wide angle lens | 28 mm — Vivitar |
| Zoom Lens | 75-205 mm zoom — Vivitar |
| Film | 50 rolls: 15 64ASA, 34 200ASA, 1 400ASA |
| Polarizer | 1 for 50mm lens |
| Waterproof carrier | 1 Sportsafe lined with foam |
| Flash unit | 1 Vivitar |
| Spare batteries | 2 sets for flash |
| Paper | 10 pads of paper |
| Pens, pencils | 10 Bics pens, 10 pencils and sharpener |
| Camera battery | 1 spare set |
| Diary | 3 books with covering |
| Binoculars | 1 pair — 7 × 35 |
| Tape recorder/player | 1 — Sony — converted to block battery |
| Cards | 2 decks |
| Backgammon/checkers | board and men |
| Cribbage board | 1 |
| Tapes | 24 prerecorded tapes |
| Birthday/Christmas | special things |
| Glue | regular for paper |
| Oil paint set | 1 regular |
| Needlepoint kit | 1 regular |
| Cross country skis | 2 pair — Splitkein |
| Cross country boots | 2 pair — Alfa |
| Cross country poles | 2 pair — Tyrol — also for hiking |
| Long socks | 2 pair |
| Day packs | 2 regular |
| Waxes | for skis — two cases Swix |
| Cork | for ski waxing |
| Wineskin | carry water for skiing trips |
| Leather | 6′ × 4′ — for repairs |
| Extra laces | 4 pair — 2 long and 2 regular |
| Snowshoes | 2 pair — Avery Brothers |
| Snowshoe boots | 2 pair — felt lined Kaufman |
| Spare liners | 2 pair for snowshoe boots |
| Snowshoe harness | 2 pair |
| Tent | 2 4-Man Timberline tents |
| Spare poles | 2 spare poles for Timberline tents |
| Backpacking stove | 1 Optimus 8R with pump and eyedropper |
| Fuel bottles | 2 Optimus 1 litre bottles |
| Pour spout | 1 — tied to one fuel bottle |
| Crazy Carpet | 1 red — for pulling loads while skiing |
| Ensolite sleeping pads | 2 long pads |
| Air-Lifts | 2 mattresses for sleeping |

| Boots | 2 pair — Raichle and Vasque |
| Snoseal | 4 tins — medium size |
| Tent vestibule | 1 for 4-man Timberline |
| Fishing rods | 2 — both collapsible |
| Reels | 2 regular |
| Lures, line, leaders | assortment of spinners and spoons |
| Planting seeds | 8 packages for garden |
| Silicone spray | 1 tin for outdoor equipment |
| Snow shovel | 1 lightweight — winter camping/cabin use |
| Watch battery | 1 for John's Watch |
| Bug jackets | 2 — Protector Brand |
| Repex | 2 small jars |
| Head nets | 2 — for when it gets unbearable |
| Sierra Cup | 1 regular |
| Books | assortment: instructional, biography, crafts, nature, history, dictionary health, medical, business, cooking |

*Food*

| Toilet paper | 1 roll per week |
| White flour | 100 pounds |
| Whole wheat flour | 50 pounds |
| Bran | 15 pounds |
| Cornmeal | 25 pounds |
| Oatmeal | 50 pounds |
| Red River cereal | 6 large boxes |
| Cream of Wheat cereal | 12 small boxes |
| Bisquick | 12 pounds |
| Wheat germ | 5 pounds |
| Brown sugar | 20 kilograms |
| White sugar | 20 kilograms |
| Pancake mix | 10 kilograms |
| Soups | 300 packages — Assorted Swiss-Knorr |
| Powdered eggs | 150 dozen-packs — E-Z Eggs |
| Beans — navy | 20 pounds |
| Beans — kidney | 5 pounds |
| Rice | 50 pounds |
| Macaroni | 20 pounds elbows |
| Spaghetti | 20 pounds |
| Lentils | 5 pounds |
| Bacon | 2 tins canned bacon |
| Dried potato mix | 12 medium boxes |
| Cheese | 56 pounds — wrapped in waxed cloth |
| Maple syrup | 2 gallons |

| | |
|---|---|
| Molasses | 4 175oz. jugs |
| Tomato paste | 48 small tins |
| Jam — strawberry | 30 pound plastic pail |
| Peanut butter — Skippy | 25 pound plastic pail |
| Honey | 6 4 pound tubs |
| Melba toast | 1 case |
| Cranberry sauce | 3 tins — special dinners |
| Lemon juice | 10 squeeze lemons |
| Drink crystals | 6 cases — 12 1 pound bags per case; 3 orange, 1 lemonade, 1 grapefruit, 1 apple juice |
| | |
| Pate — chicken | 24 small tins |
| Pate — ham | 24 small tins |
| Pate — liver | 24 small tins |
| Tuna | 1 case of 48 medium size tins |
| Salmon | 1 case of 24 1 pound tins |
| Sardines | 25 small tins |
| Corned beef | 24 medium tins |
| Klik/Kam | 24 tins |
| Carob chips | 30 pounds |
| Chocolate | 20 pounds of hot cocoa mix |
| Peanuts | 35 pounds of Salted peanuts |
| Raisins | 36 pounds |
| Prunes | 33 pounds |
| Soya nuts | 5 pounds |
| Caramels | 5 pounds |
| Dates | 5 pounds |
| Dried apricots | 5 pounds |
| Dried peaches | 3 pounds |
| Chocolate bars | 24 Mars Bars |
| Gum | 72 packages — sugarless gum |
| Coffee creamer | 25 pounds |
| Freeze-dried foods: | All Hardee Brand |
| Bulk Chicken | 5 large packages — 50 servings |
| Bulk beef | 5 large packages — 50 servings |
| Bulk mushroom | 5 large packages — 50 servings |
| Bulk peas | 5 large packages — 50 servings |
| Bulk corn | 5 large packages — 50 servings |
| Bulk green beans | 5 large packages — 50 servings |
| Beef steaks | 6 two serving pouches |
| Pork chops | 12 2 serving pouches |
| Carrots | 36 2 servings pouches |
| Applesauce | 12 2 serving pouches |

| | |
|---|---|
| Chicken stew | 12 2 serving pouches |
| Rice and chicken | 12 2 serving pouches |
| Beef stew | 12 2 serving pouches |
| Beef stroganoff | 12 2 serving pouches |
| Chili con carne | 12 2 serving pouches |
| Barbeque sauce mix | 20 packages |
| Spaghetti sauce mix | 24 packages |
| Chili sauce mix | 20 packages |
| Spices | Assortment: chili, garlic, cinnamon, savory, dill, rosemary, curry, cumin, mustard, pepper |
| | |
| Baking soda | 12 medium boxes |
| Baking powder | 1 very large tin |
| Yeast | 1 very large tin |
| Parmesan cheese | 5 pounds |
| Vanilla | 4 large jars |
| Canned hams | 6 large tins |
| Canned chickens | 3 large tins |
| Pudding | 1 case — butterscotch |
| Cheesecake | No-Bake — 6 packages |
| Peel for Christmas cake | 5 pounds |
| Pumpkin | 2 large tins |
| Mincemeat | 2 large tins |
| Plum pudding | 2 packages |
| Mung seeds | 5 pounds for sprouting |
| S.O.S pads | 360 pads |
| Liquid soap | Two 175oz. containers |
| J-Cloths | 6 large packages |
| Washing soap | 48 bars of Ivory — it floats |
| Washing soap | 12 bars of Pear's — Joanne |
| Toothpaste | 24 large tubes |
| Green garbage bags | 12 packages of 12 bags each |
| Plastic bags | 200 assorted — canoeing and backpacking |
| Shampoo | 12 bottles |
| Laundry soap | 25 pounds |
| Coffee | 36 packages — 160 servings each |
| Tea | 200 2-cup bags |
| Margarine | 2 30 pound pails |
| Cooking oil | 30 pounds |
| Salt | 30 pounds |
| Milko | 80 pounds |
| Popcorn | 5 pounds |
| Baby oil | 6 large containers |

| Vaseline | 6 small containers |
| Licorice | 1 case |
| Ketchup | 1 large tin |
| Crisco | 6 large tins |
| Ovaltine | 6 jars |
| Tampons | 12 large boxes |